Gnomic Literature
in Bible and Apocrypha

Gnomic Literature
in Bible and Apocrypha

With Special Reference to
the Gnomic Fragments and Their Bearing on
the Proverb Collections

By
GERSON B. LEVI, Ph. D.

WIPF & STOCK · Eugene, Oregon

Wipf and Stock Publishers
199 W 8th Ave, Suite 3
Eugene, OR 97401

Gnomic Literature in Bible and Apocrypha
With Special Reference to the Gnomic Fragments
and Their Bearing on the Proverb Collections
By Gerson B. Levi
ISBN 13: 978-1-55635-648-3
Publication date 10/2/2007

Introduction

The fragments of the Massoretic text of the Bible, that are gnomic in character, though some of them have been incidentally noted by the commentators, have never been collected. The attempt is here made, therefore, to gather as many as could be recognized and accounted gnomic. When the mass is collected and examined, it serves, it is believed, to make a new historical background for the larger canonical and post-canonical books of the gnomic series. Being in many cases the products of popular speech, and dealing with subjects and in terms unused by the literary men—poets, prophets and pragmatic historians—these fragments possess a vocabulary comparatively rich in hapax legomena. The comparative study of these fragments will, moreover, prove that the dates for the beginnings of literary activity in old Israel must be placed further back, as against the current notion and tendency to bring down and to postpone the rise of the literary craft. At least, the discussion of the passages in Amos, in particular, and the fragments and quotations in Hosea is aimed to show that the gnomic literature must be presumed to have been in a flourishing condition and to have been possessed of forms, hitherto assumed to have been late in origin, before the day of the earliest literary prophets. Besides a preprophetic prophetic school there was also a preprophetic gnomic school and the literary prophets drew materials and forms from both schools. The form that by the commentators is everywhere made prima facie evidence of lateness of composition is here shown to be, of necessity, one of the very early forms.

The attempt has been made, further, from the study of the fragments extant, to establish the presence of a literature to some extent heretical. Because it was heretical it was antagonized and later destroyed by the victorious school of the prophets. Nevertheless, some traces still remain to speak of the wide influence that these sayings of the popular phrase makers had upon the people. Through this examination, it is hoped that some gaps left by the study of the independent groups of proverbs as found in the Wisdom Literature will be filled up, and the knowledge of the old masters—the wise men—be increased.

There still remains the pleasant task of acknowledging my indebtedness to Professor Morris Jastrow, Jr., for the many helpful suggestions given both as to the method and the materials of the work.

GERSON B. LEVI.

1. Extent of the Literature

Two whole books, one in the canon proper and one in the Apocrypha, are given over to the literature of proverbs, maxims and wise sayings. But the literature is far more extensive than even this would indicate. For scattered throughout the Bible, there are snatches and frequently quite large selections of such gnomic material. Such selections we should naturally expect to find first of all in the division of the so-called Wisdom Literature. The Book of Ecclesiastes falls quite often from the plane of the Cynic Philosopher either to quote or to coin a proverb—1, 15; 2, 14; 3, 1-8; 4, 2-3; 5, 2:6:9; 6, 9-12;*[1] 7, 1-13; 8:9, 16-18; 10, 1-13; 10, 18:20b; etc. Job has a number of such passages—2, 4;*[2] 5, 5-6; 5, 19-23; 5, 7; 14, 6-10; 14, 18-19; 15, 20-35; 12, 5-7; 12, 11-25; 34, 3; 18, 5-20; 20, 5; 27, 14-23; 14, 28; 31, 40. But besides these, which occur in groups and are to be found in the Wisdom Books, there are fragments to be found in the historical, poetic and prophetic sections. They are perhaps for this reason even more important for our study.

Under the heading משל, (compare the Arabic *m th l* "similitude" and the Assyrian "mashalu" = "to be like"*[3] and "tamshilu" = "a likeness"*[4] and see Isaiah 46,5 למי תדמיוני ותשיו ותמשלני "To whom will you liken me and making equal compare me," and Isaiah 14, 10 אלינו נמשלת "Thou art become like one of us") we find in the Bible proverbs in the real sense of the word. "The fathers have eaten sour grapes and the teeth of the children stand on edge" אבות יאכלו בסר ושיני הבנים תקהינה Ezekiel 18, 2. This proverb is taken from the mouth of the people. Popular theology, it would seem, recognized the condition of hereditary taint and made the assumption that the sins of the fathers weighed heavily upon the shoulders of the children. The notion was repugnant to Ezekiel, who enforces, on the contrary, the principle that man shall suffer for his own misdeeds alone and be rewarded for his own merits. It is to be noted that this proverb has a history. Jeremiah, too, deals with it, (31, 28) although he knows it in a slightly different form.*[5] He also finds it necessary to combat its perverted theology. In the Midrash Rabba, Vayikra, Tazria, 15, 5 *[6] the proverb is brought into connection with a similar statement in Lamentations 3, 5—"Our fathers sinned and are no more, but we must bear their iniquities." In Jeremiah, the proverb is introduced by the phrase לא יאמרו עוד which might best be rendered "people will no longer say." The popular origin of the proverb will be even clearer when the negative form of the introduction is changed to the positive. It then becomes a parallel to 1 Sam 19, 24 על כן יאמרו. In Ezekiel, it is introduced by the longer formula מה לכם מושלים את המשל הזה "Why do you make this proverb?" One other proverb is introduced in this double style. The story of Saul's stay with the prophet Samuel at Ramah gave rise according to one version, in 1 Sam 19, 24, to the proverb הגם שאול בנביאים "Is Saul also among the prophets?" But in 1 Sam 10, 12 the proverb is given in connection with an earlier event in the life of Saul, and a more circumstantial attempt is made to give an explanation to a proverb which lay back of both versions and had already, at the time of the compiler of the book, as we have it before us, become dark.*[7] Whatever the later application, the proverb must have had its origin in the feeling of incongruity in Saul's companionship with the prophets. The difference in the mind of the later writer acted to the disadvantage of Saul, because the proverb in his day could not help being tinged with the newer value and dignity of the prophetic school and the rejection of the king by that school. So while the proverb originally expressed surprise that a man like Saul should be found in the company of wandering enthusiasts, it later expressed surprise that Saul should have been found worthy of companionship with the seers. In 1 Sam 10, 12, the proverb is introduced by על כן היתה למשל "Therefore it became a proverb."

In the prophetic literature the following are to be noted. Beginning with Isaiah, we have in 1, 3 what is evidently an old proverb ידע שור קנהו וחמור אבוס בעליו "The ox knoweth his master and the ass his owner's crib." What follows is given by the prophet as a contrast and is his own elaboration of the theme of the proverb. Jeremiah has a long development of the same theme*[8] but there it is not worked out in the nature of a proverb. Perhaps the short phrases כסכה בכרם, כמלונה במקשה, כעיר נצורה "As a hut in a vineyard," "as a lodge in a cucumber field," "as a fenced city" should be added to the list of proverbial phrases. Isaiah 10, 15 היתפאר הגרזן על החצב בו אם יתגדל המשור על מניפו "Shall the axe boast itself over him that heweth therewith, or shall the saw magnify itself against him that swingeth it." Here too the continuation is an amplification of the intention of the proverb, but in the prophet's style. 22, 13 for the sake of the later proverbial use—אכל ושתה כי מחר נמות "eat and drink for tomorrow we die," ought to be included. Isaiah 28, 14ff has been generally misunderstood. The Septuagint *[9] translates אנשי לצון משלי העם הזה by ἄνδρες τεθλιμμένοι, καὶ ἄρχοντες τοῦ | λαοῦ τούτου. The Targum has the same rendering גברין רשיעין שלטוני עמא הדין Duhm*[10] has" Darum hört das wort Jahves, ihr Männer des Spottes, Beherrscher dieses Volkes da, das in Jerusalem ist" Marti*[11] renders the verse in the same way keeping the idea of the rulers and the scoffers. Cheyne*[12] has the following note—"Jehovah pronounces judgment. He addresses—not the king who is passed over in silence in most of the Hezekian discourses of

Isaiah—but the rulers, the politicians. These are designated men of scorn. The title scoffers seems to be given in Proverbs to those who opposed or despised the counsels of the wise men and broke through the restraints of law and religion." Dillman*[13] renders "Männer des Spottes" and "die Beherrscher des Volkes." Orelli*[14] translates "ihr Spottbeflissenen, ihr Herrscher dieses Volkes." Hitzig*[15] has this rendering "Darum so hört das Wort Jahves ihr Spottredner, Herrscher dieses Volkes." These are therefore unanimous in regarding משלי as a form of משל "to rule." But when the phrase is so rendered it is out of harmony with the preceding section with which it is in every other way to be connected. There has not been a single word concerning the rulers in the previous verse. Furthermore the connection has been lost just through this rendering. The prophet has been speaking of the fact that they who should have given the people advice were spiritually unsound and incapable of correct judgment. Priest and prophet are drunk. What they said was all wrong. They mock the true prophet's teaching, jeer at his language קו לקו צו לצו. Now comes his answer to them. In this answer "Moshele ha'am" can only mean "Those who make proverbs for the people." That the root משל can be, and as a matter of fact, actually is, used in this sense, the introductory formula to the proverb in Ezekiel 18, 2 shows. By this rendering of "Moshele ha'am" the difficulties with the "anshe lazon" are also removed, for that also stands in some technical sense. If we accept the interpretation of the commentators above quoted, we have in the text a combination of "men of scorn" and "rulers of the people" and while of course any two things can be connected by and, it is hard to say just what class or classes this combination covers. But with the rendering above suggested, we are prepared to see that the prophet is here using לצון in a secondary sense and is depending upon the ingenuity of the hearers or readers to fathom his meaning. The basic notion of לצון is, we must presume, perfectly familiar to his hearers. The associations with other terms for proverbs are also familiar. He therefore uses לצון intentionally not in the sense of scorn or scoffing, but in the sense of wrong proverbial philosophy. The opposition between the wise man and the אנשי לצון is indicated by Proverbs 29, 8 where the meaning has again been missed and the translation "men of scorn" given instead of "unwise advisers." Frankenberg*[16] has "Spötter versetzen die Stadt in Aufruhr." Wildeboer*[17] translates "Männer des Spottes" refers to Isaiah 28, 14 but makes no further use of the reference and allows the phrase to stand as it is. Toy*[18] renders "Unscrupulous men kindle discord in the city." But there is in none of the interpretations a proper antithesis between the term אנשי לצון and the חכמים "wise men" of the second part of the verse. Further, the opposition between the product of theWise men— חכמה and the product of the opposite type of man לצון is given in Proverbs 1, 21-22.*[19] The prophet has amplified the original statement in Isaiah 28, 14ff as he did in 1, 3 and 10, 15—"Ye have said 'We have made a covenant with death (that is that it should not touch us) and with sheol we have made a pact'." This they can say but they would hardly end "We have made a lie our refuge and in falsehood have we found our hiding place." That is the prophet's mocking continuation of their "wisdom."

Isaiah 28, 20 has this proverb— כי קצר המצע מהשתרע והמסכה צרה מהתכנם "Perhaps a proverbial expression for a state of painful uneasiness" Cheyne*[20] and a similar statement of Duhm*[21] attest the conceded proverbial character of the verse. Radak, too, recognized the general proverbial character and gave it the same interpretation. The Targum goes its own way and is worthless here as a check on the text. Cheyne looks upon the verse as an interpolation because of the Aramaism, but the proverbs drawn from the popular speech would be apt to be tinged with this Aramaism and the proverb can therefore be a genuine and integral part of the text. It does look as if the מחתכנם should be read מחתנכם. In the only other passage where the word מסכה occurs the verb that goes with it is the one formed from the same root. That change sets aside all the difficulties natural with the renderings to gather oneself together or with the necessity or forced comparison with root נגז (Duhm). The Septuagint goes its own way and gives no hint as to the Hebrew text that it had.

Isaiah 28, 23-29 is a gnomic section recognizable both by the subject matter as well as by style and the use of תושיה and עצה words familiar to the gnomic writers. Tushiyah is found only twice outside the Wisdom Literature: in this passage and in Micah 6, 9.*[22] Eẓah, however, is more frequently found.*[23] Isaiah 32, particularly verses 6-8—"For the worthless person ever speaketh villainy and his heart will work injustice" is most certainly gnomic. Isaiah 33, 13-16 is a parallel to Psalm 15.*[24] Isaiah 37, 3—"for the children are come to the birth, and there is not strength to bring forth" is proverbial in character and can be used to indicate any process carried almost to completion and then failing of final accomplishment. The theme of Isaiah 40, 12-16 is a favorite one of the Wisdom School. It is paralleled by Job 38, 5 and by Proverbs 4, 1ff. Isaiah 45, 9-10 is a parallel to 10, 15—"Shall the clay say to the potter 'what doest thou' and thy work 'he has no hands'." The next verse is probably a continuation of the proverb. 49, 15—"Can a woman forget her babe;" 66, 8—"Can a land be born in one day, or can a nation be born in one instant" are both proverbs. 49, 24—היקח מגבור מלקוח ואם שבי צדיק ימלט requires a slight change of text. צדיק in b has no parallel for such a usage and besides the explanation of the proverb given by the prophet himself (consisting of an assertion answering the question in the affirmative and using all the words of the question with the one exception of צדיק) demands that we read עריץ instead of צדיק.*[25]

Jeremiah 8, 22—"Is there no balm in Gilead" might be included for the sake of the fact that later it became a proverbial phrase. Jeremiah 8, 7 has already been referred to as an artificial working out and development of a proverbial theme. Back of the phrases in both Isaiah and Jeremiah there is the observed natural sagacity of animals in finding their way to and in recognizing their home. Jeremiah 9, 22-23 is decidedly gnomic. "Let not the wise man boast*[26] of his wisdom, and let not the strong man boast of his strength, nor let the rich man boast of his wealth. Only in this let him who would boast—in understanding and knowing me." How gnomic this is can be seen from the naturalness with which the elaborated passage fits into the Genizah Gnomic Fragments.*[27] 13, 23—"Can the Ethiopian change his skin or the leopard his spots" is a proverb with an immediate application—"so can you, taught to do evil, not do good." 17, 5-8 has gnomic material having some affinities with Ps 1.*[28] 18, 6 has the figure of the clay in the hands of the potter. 18, 14—a proverb of natural phenomena—"Doth the snow of Lebanon ever quit the rock of the field, or do the far-coming cold flowing waters ever fail." Perhaps the short phrases "as Tabor among the hills" and as "Carmel out of the sea" should be included.*[29] 23, 28—מה לתבן את הבר "What hath the straw to do with the corn" is clearly proverbial. Jeremiah 48, 43—a statement of general destruction פחד ופחת ופח is to be compared with Isaiah 24, 17-18, which seems to come first in time, and Lamentations 3, 47 where only the first two are used and two others substituted for the third. Amos 5, 18 has the succession but has the details given more elaborately. See also for a similar thought in Job 8, 15 ישען על ביתו ולא יעמד יחזיק בו ולא יקום. Jeremiah 49, 9—"If the gleaners had come to thee, would they not have left gleanings, if spoilers of the night, would they not destroy (only) to their fill" is taken from Obadiah 5.

In Ezekiel 11, 3 there is evidently a proverb. האומרים לא בקרוב בנות בתים, היא הסיר ואנחנו הבשר. The intention is clear though all, the details are not. The men of Jerusalem are speaking of themselves as being the flesh in the pot—a figure indicating the city. But whether safety or absolute hopelessness of escape is indicated can be argued.*[30] The same figure of the pot, this time in the longer form of the allegory, is to be found in Ezekiel 24, 3ff. What the prophet expressly calls a "mashal" is given in 12, 22 יארכו הימים ואבד כל חזון "The days are lengthening (in the sense 'time is passing') and every vision is lost (in the sense of 'not being realized')." This is a popular saying quoted by Ezekiel for the express purpose of contradiction. The first mashal reads יארכו הימים ואבד כל חזון—a two membered saying. The answer to it is intended naturally to preserve the same structure of a two membered saying, but as the text stands it fails to preserve such structure. To establish this Ewald*[31] reads ועבר basing the emendation on Isaiah 28, 21. Cornill*[32] has ובא "and it shall come to pass." Bertholet*[33] suggests וגבר "it shall prevail and shall hasten on." Kretzchmar*[34] has ומהר. The objection to all of these proposed emendations is that they all of them refer to the actual fulfillment of the prophecy. About an actual fulfillment there cannot be any question. When the prophecies shall have been fulfilled there will not be any room for doubt. If the people were willing to wait for that test, these emendations would describe and satisfy the conditions. But that is not the feeling of the people. What they question is this. The time is passing by and in this lengthening of the days, the prophecies have, so to speak, lost effect and slipped up on the way. The prophet insists that such is not the case. They are still in force. I read therefore ועמד. For the possibility of such a use of "amad" see Ps. 102, 27 where the other word "abad" is actually used as its opposite תמח יאבדו ואתה תעמוד and compare Jer. 32, 14 למען יעמדו ימים רבים Isaiah 66, 22 כן יעמד זרעכם = to endure and see also Ps. 33, 11 עצת יהוה לעולם תעמוד and Ps. 33, 9 הוא צוה ויעמד. We read therefore קרבו תימים ועמד כל חזון. Ezekiel 16, 44 כאמה בתה—"as the mother is, so is the daughter" is called a mashal in the text.

Hosea 4, 11 זנות ויין ותירוש יקח לב—"Whoredom and wine and new wine steal away the heart" is undoubtedly a proverb.*[35] לב is used here in the wisdom-literature sense. See Job 8, 10; 9, 4; 12, 3; 12, 24; Pro 6, 32.*[36] Hosea 4, 1b כי אין אמת ואין חסד ואין אלהים בארץ if not an actual quotation is rightly called by Harper*[37] a "remnant of proverbial literature." Hosea 4, 14d ועם לא יבין ילבט is perhaps the second half of a regular proverb.*[38] The stem LBT is found only here and in Proverbs 10, 8. 10. The verse here in Hosea hangs together very loosely and the ending is clearly not a part of the general structure of the sentence. It is therefore to be looked upon as a quotation. Perhaps Hosea 6, 3 כשחר נכון מוצאו ויבא כגשם לנו כמלקוש יורה ארץ ought to be included as ought also 6, 4b וחסדכם כענן בקר וכטל משכים הלך. Hosea 6, 6 has relationships with passages in the Proverbial Literature and in the historical books—"For kindness have I desired and not sacrifice and the knowledge of God more than burnt offerings." (Of the theological imputations more, when the concepts of the Proverbial literature are dealt with). Hosea 8,7a—"For they sow the wind and a whirlwind shall they reap" is a proverb. Similar is the sentiment expressed in Hosea 10, 13—"Ye have plowed evil, iniquity shall ye reap, ye shall eat the fruit of lying." Hosea 10, 12 has something of the personal tone of the wise man teaching. Hosea 14, 10 is another gnomic passage—"Who is wise and will understand these things, understanding them that he may know them, for the ways of the Lord are right, the righteous shall walk in them and the transgressors shall stumble through them." Finally we have Hosea 13, 2—"Of them it is said 'They sacrifice men and kiss calves'."

Amos has a number of passages which ought to be considered besides the three-four-numbered passages which will come up for consideration later. Amos 3, 3—"Will two go together except they have appointed a time." The Septuagint*[39] suggests the reading נודעו instead of the present Hebrew text of נועדו. This is followed by Marti*[40] who gives the reason that two orientals would not walk together unless they knew each other. But this reason would operate even more in case we read with the present Hebrew text נועדו. Besides that, נועדו is the more difficult reading and ought not to be set aside too lightly. Amos 3, 4—"Will the lion roar in the forest and yet have no prey, will the young lion give forth his voice from his cave except that he have caught." 3, 5—"Can a bird fall in a snare upon the earth when there is no gin set for him, is ever a snare taken up from the ground when it hath caught nothing." 3, 6—"Will a trumpet be blown in a city and the people not be afraid, will there be evil in a city and the Lord have not done it." The structure of this sentence is not as parallelistic as was the structure of the other two. We propose the change of vowels and read רעת from the root רעע—"to shake, to quake" then "an earthquake." The guttural would be responsbile for the change of vowel. The formation would be the same as סבת from סבב. Amos 5, 18—"As a man fleeing from a lion and a bear meets him and he comes into the house and leans his hand against the wall and a snake bites him" is the complete form of what in Jeremiah was given first in short and then in longer form—see Jeremiah 48, 43. Amos 6, 12—"Can horses run on the flinty rock or can a man plow the sea with oxen?" This of course accepts the emendation*[41] of breaking babekarim into two words babakar yam. Amos 6, 13—"Who say 'is it not by our own strength that we have taken ourselves horns'," i.e. our supremacy is the fruit of the labor of our own hands, is hardly a proverb. It is merely a popular claim.

Micah 2, 4 has a passage that is in the text called a mashal, but from the contents it borders very closely on the dirge and from the structure of it, it appears to be a Kinah.*[42] "We are wasted, the portion of my people he hath changed, how hath he removed it from me, instead of restoring he hath divided my fields."

Habakuk 1, 14 כרמש לא מושל בו has affinities with Proverbs 6, 6 אשר אין לה קצין שוטר ומושל Habakuk 2, 6—Here the use of mashal falls in line with the use of it made in Isaiah 14, not as a proverb but as a taunting speech.

Jonah 4, 10 שבן לילה היה ובן לילה אבד is undoubtedly a quotation from some proverb which had to deal with the shortness and uncertainty of human life.

Haggai 1, 6 is only distantly gnomic but the last member —והמשתכר משתכר אל צרור נקוב sounds like a proverb.

The Book of Psalms stands on the borderland of many varieties of composition. It passes from the lyrical to the historical and to the didactic. It is to be expected therefore that it should be rich in proverbial material. 7,15—"Behold he travaileth with iniquity, hath conceived wrong and hath begotten falsehood." The subject matter of this proverb is handled frequently and with the same application. See Hosea 8, 7; 10, 13 as well as Job 15, 35 הרה עמל וילד און ובטנם תכין מרמה The next two verses (Psalms 7, 16-17) are undoubtedly proverbs. Maimonides in his commentary to the Pirke Aboth—"The Chapters of the Fathers"—explains (Chapter 2 paragraph 6) verse 16 by the Rabbinic saying—"Bemidah sheadam moded modedin lo" "As a man measures they measure unto him." This saying is quoted also in the Seder Eliyahu Zuta (Friedmann edition, page 170). For the same notion see Ben Sira 27, 25-27. A similar notion is found in Ps. 9, 16 טבעו גוים בשחת עשו

ברשת זו טמנו נלכדה רגלם and in 35, 8— ורשתו אשר טמן תלכדו See also Proverbs 26, 27 כרה שחת בו יפול וגלל אבן אליו תשוב See also Ec 10, 8 חופר גומץ בו יפול ופרץ גדר ישכנו נחש. The rabbinic saying is paralleled by the New Testament Mat. 7, 2. For quotations other than these see Perle (Oẓar Leshon Hachamim, Warsaw 1900 p, 86, no. 1245). Psalms 18, 25-28 has a gnomic passage paralleled by 2 Sam 22, 25-27 with the difference of a few minor text changes. 30, 10 היודך עפר היגיד אמתך and 6, 6— כי אין במות זכרך בשאול מי יודה לך and 88, 11-13—"Wilt thou display thy wonders to the dead, shall the departed arise and thank thee. Shall thy wonders be acknowledged in the darkness, and thy righteousness in the land of forgetfulness. Shall they kindness be related in the grave, thy faithfulness in the place of corruption" belong to a proverbial notion which must have gone the rounds and must have been worked up into longer or shorter forms, but all with the same thought "Can the dead speak." Ps. 32, 8-10 is clearly gnomic in character, as is to be seen from the introductory verbs אשכילך אורך. Briggs*[43] has this to say of the passage, it is—"in accordance with the legal attitude of mind subsequent to Nehemiah." But there is here no legal implication at all. Askileclah is distinctively a gnomic word. It is a denominative from Sechel. For the gnomic use of sechel compare Proverbs 21, 11—ובהשכל לחכם יקח דעת and Ps. 94, 8 בינו בערים בעם וכסילים מתי תשכילו. Ehrlich*[44] would change eni into beni. This would of course carry out even still further the gnomic character of the passage. But despite the inviting emendation, since the acceptance of the Septuagint*[45] reading makes sense possible, eni will have to be retained. Moreover the LXX reading is supported by Proverbs 16, 30 עצה עיניו. The last three words בל קרוב אליך look like a gloss. Ps. 33 is gnomic. So also is Ps. 34. In this Psalm verses 12-15 are highly interesting. Here the Psalmist intentionally passes over to the style of the "Moshel meshalim" or the "Methaken meshalim" and calls out as the proverbialist, addressing his hearers, real or imaginary, as sons—"banim"—and gives them instruction exactly as the book of Proverbs pictures. Baethgen*[46] "Die Gemeinde redet ihre Kinder d.i. angehörigen an. Ebenso spricht die personificierte Weisheit Pro 8, 32" misses the mark. The relationship between the literature of Proverbs and of Psalms is even closer than Duhm's*[47] "errinert an die Proverbien wie so manches andere in Ps. 25; 34." The selection gives a suggestion as to the methods of the teachers not indicated as clearly in the confessedly Proverbial books. It certainly looks as if the answer to the 13th verse would be looked for eagerly by the listeners, and it is equally as certain that they did not expect the answer that really was given. Talmud Babli, Abodah Zarah 19b has this purposely enigmatic style heightened by making the speaker disguise the fact that it is a quotation that he is about to give. Therefore it has the question "Who desires life" in Aramaic. The answer is the quotation from the Psalms.*[48] The same indication of the relationship of personal interest between teacher and pupil is given in Ps 32, 8. Ps 37 is also gnomic but note the proverb in verse 16—טוב מעט לצדיק מהמון רשעים רבים. The text here, however requires some emendation.*[49] The personal relationship is to be seen again in verse 35 when the didactic element comes strongly forward. The same didactic spirit is to be seen in Psalm 50, 16-21. Here God himself is the teacher. A terse saying part way across the borders of proverbland is to be found in Ps 69, 5—"Those who hate me for no reason are more numerous than the 'hair of my head'." Psalm 78 is another didactic Psalm. In the preface the writer promises to speak "meshalim" and "ḥidoth." אפתחה במשל פי, אביעה חידות מני קדם. That ḥidoth was used in a rather diluted sense is clear from this passage. It gradually fell into a class with mashal and meliẓah and all of the phrases melted down finally into meaning a didactic poem. This is the case also in Psalm 49, 5—אטה למשל אזני אפתחה בכינור חידתי. Ps. 90, 10—"The days of our years are seventy years and if with strength are eighty years" has passed into a proverb. Ps. 89, 49—"What man will live and not see death who will deliver his soul from death (from Sheol) Selah" if not in itself a proverb could easily be made into one. Ps. 94, 8-10 בינו בוערים כעם וכסילים מתי תשכילו; הנוטע אזן הלא ישמע אם יוצר עין חלא יביט; חיסר גוים חלא יוכיח המלמד אדם דעת; are undoubtedly proverbs. The last couplet is not complete. There is no authority for the emendation but it does look as if it ought to be completed by a statement like חלא יבין. It is to be noticed that the introduction to this little proverbial section is to be found in the preceding verse (8) and there the form of "Taskilu" is used—the form which was taken by Briggs*[50] as the unfailing sign of the legalistic period of Nehemiah. Ps 111 and 112 are gnomic Psalms and belong together. They have parallelisms in the construction, have phrases in common (עמדת לעד and verses 111, 3 and 112, 3). Ps. 105, 106 and 107 belong to the didactic class. Notice particularly in Ps. 107, 43 the appeal to the wise men—"Mi ḥacham veyishmor eleh." Perhaps 118, 22—"The stone which the builders rejected hath become the corner stone" ought to be included for the sake of its gnomic possibilities. The same might be said of verses 8 and 9—"It is better to trust in the Lord than to trust in man. It is better to trust in the Lord than to trust in princes." Ps 132, 4—"If I shall allow my eyes to sleep and mine eyelids slumber" is probably a quotation from Proverbs 6, 4—"Do not give sleep to thine eyes and slumber to thine eyelids." (See Baethgen*[51] "Für den David in den Mund gelegten Schwur verwendet der Dichter hier ein Citat aus Pro 6, 4.") Ps 119 is alphabetic and gnomic as is Ps. 145.

Song of Songs 8, 6ff has a proverbial passage—"For strong as death is love, worse than death is its pain. The mighty waters cannot quench it and rivers cannot flood it away. If a man should give all the wealth of his house for love they would scorn him."*[52]

In the historical books of the Bible the following are to be noted. Joshua 6, 26—"With his first born shall he lay the foundations and with his youngest shall he set up the gates." The verse is doubtless an old remnant.*[53] It must have come from an old collection akin perhaps to the "sefer hayashar" as later quoted in Joshua itself. The saying is assumed by the narrator of Kings 1:16, 34. It had become a proverbial statement of the costliness of the rebuilding of Jericho. But back of this there is the attempt to explain what quite possibly happened in the building of the city—the immuring of a human victim.*[54]

Judges 9, 2b—"and ye shall remember that 'I am your flesh and blood' " hints at the existence of a proverb which parallels the English formula "Blood is thicker than water." Another short proverb is given in Judges 8, 21—"As the man is, so is his strength." Here the reason for a definite line of action is given by the apt quotation of a proverb. The form of this one is the same as the very short one of Ezekiel 1, 16, 44 where the presence of a proverb is indicated however by the word "mashal." The closing statement of Judges (also Judges 17, 6) could easily pass over into a proverb. See Talmud Babli Sotah 47b where the phrase has clearly become a proverbial idiom. "When 'every-man-did-what-was-right-in-his-own-eyes' multiplied, the humble (in the sense of the undeserving) were exalted and the exalted (deserving) were humbled." The riddle in Judges 14 is usually counted among the proverbs or in the mashal literature, but the answer of Samson "If you had not plowed with my heifer you would not have discovered my riddle" ought also be included. It was so recognized by the ancient Jewish commentators. Ḳimḥi (in loco) says "al derech mashal." Rashi (in loco) has "mashal hu." For Judges

12, 3 ואשימה נפשי בכפי "I took my life in my hands," compare Job 13, 14—"Why should I carry my flesh in my teeth and why should I place my life in my hands" and 1 Sam. 19, 5—"And he put his life into his hand and he smote the Philistine."

1 Sam 24, 13 David quotes an old proverb "mashal kadmoni"—from the wicked proceedeth wickedness." 1 Sam 15, 22—"Behold to obey is better than to sacrifice and to attend is more acceptable than the fat of rams" has many relatives in the literature acknowledged proverbial. Proverbs 21, 3—"To exercise righteousness and justice is more acceptable to the Lord than sacrifice" and Sira 34, 20—"The Lord is not pleased with the offerings of the wicked, neither is he pacified for sin by the multitudes of sacrifices" and Hosea 6, 6—"For kindness have I desired and not sacrifices, and the knowledge of God more than burnt offerings" have the same notion. 1 Sam 15, 23 "The sin of witchcraft is rebellion, and idolatry and image worship is stubbornness." 1 Sam 26, 20 has two proverbial expressions. The first is found also in 1 Sam 24, 15 ("After whom is the King of Israel gone forth, whom art thou pursuing, after a dead dog, after a flea"). The second "as one hunts the partridge on the hills" is found only here.*[55] For the use of כלב in the derogatory sense see 2 Sam 9, 8—"What is thy servant that thou hast turned toward a dead dog as myself" and 16, 9—"Why should this dead dog curse my lord the King." Of 1 Sam 25, 25 כשמו כן הוא "He is as his name," later usage has made a proverb. The LXX helps us to complete the proverb of 1 Sam 16, 7. As the Massoretic text stands it is not complete. The LXX*[56] seems to have had before it a Hebrew text which read כי לא אשר יראה האדם יראה יהוה. 1 Sam 14, 6—"For there is not hindrance unto the Lord to save by many or by few" has its parallel, though it is possible that this passage inspired the one in 1 Mac. 3, 18—"It is no hard matter for many to be shut up in the hands of the few,

and with the God of Heaven it is all one, to deliver with a great multitude, or a small company" and in 2 Mac 15, 27—"calleth upon the Lord that worketh wonders, knowing that victory cometh not by arms but even as it seemeth good to Him. He giveth it to such as are worthy." The noun מעצור occurs only here, as far as the canonical books are concerned. In a passage in Ben Sira evidently influenced by this one it occurs again, see Ben Sira 39, 18 ואין מעצור לתשועתו. 1 Sam 3, 20—"From Dan to Beer Sheba" is surely a proverbial phrase.

2 Sam 5, 8—Here there is a lame attempt to connect a priestly provision, tradition of which is still current in the later Halachah (see Mishnah Hagigah 1, 1 the form of the Mishnah showing that it belongs to a very early period in the development of the Halachah—"All are obliged to appear—i.e. at the festival time in Jerusalem—except the deaf, the blind, the mentally deficient, the minor, the lame, the sick, the aged, etc.) as to who shall and who shall not come into the temple, with the taking of the hill from the Jebusites.*[57] The explanation is omitted in 1 Ch 11, 6. 2 Sam 14, 14, I render as follows: (a) is a proverb "We shall all of us die" (referring not to Absalom nor to Ammon but to David himself). "We are as water thrown upon the ground." The next phrase ולא ישא אלהים נפש is an amplification of the first statement—"Not one will escape death." The conclusion therefore is a natural one. "Therefore let the king devise plans so that the exile be not driven away farther. 2 Sam 19, 4 may be a proverb "As people ashamed, steal away when they fly from the battle." Of the ancient saying in 2 Sam 20, 18 quoted by a woman described as a hachamah the proverbial value is slight though it is interesting as pointing to Abel as a seat of early Jewish tradition.

1 Kings 20, 11 has the terse reply—"Let not the man who puts on [his armor] boast as he who has taken it off."*[58] 1 Kings 12, 10 is evidently a proverb. The double assonance

קטני עבה ממתני אבי points to the same fact. When the king himself speaks, his language is not in the laconic style of the proverb. 2 Kings 21, 13 the figure of drying and then turning over again to dry more thoroughly might also be included. 1 K. 14, 15 כאשר ינוד הקנה במים is a little more than a simile.

In later times the intimate acquaintance with the Hebrew text of the Bible made proverbs of passages not really originally intended as such. For example, Deut 14, 14 ואת כל עורב למינו could from its position in the dietary laws, never have been intended as a proverb, yet it is used as the equivalent of the English "Birds of a feather flock together" or in the words of Ben Sira 27, 9—כל עוף למינו ישכן "Birds of a feather nest together" (quoted in Talmud Babli Baba Kama 92b) and כל הבשר יאהב מינו "every beast loveth his like." Emanuel of Rome (See Maḥbereth Emanuel, p 46 Lemberg Edition) has a poem in which the answer to a series of questions is given by a Biblical quotation rhyming with the question." מדוע נמצא פלני תמיד עם פלני שכנו "Why is so and so found continually in the company of such and such his neighbor?" and the answer is "כל עורב למינו." So the saying in Genesis—"It is not good for man to be alone became a proverb. Likewise "the skin of the teeth" of Job 19, 20. So Zechariah 4, 6 "not by strength nor by might but by my spirit" is already half way towards the boundary of proverbland. The same can be said of Zechariah 10, 3—"Upon the shepherds was mine anger kindled and upon the rams shall I visit (my wrath)." Habakuk 2, 4—"And the righteous man shall live by his faith" is near the border. Ps. 69, 5, already quoted, belongs to this class.

The fable has two representatives in Biblical Literature, of which the longer one in Judges 9, 8-15 is carried out to a length which shows that this form of composition must have been cultivated and must have been thoroughly intelligible to the ordinary audience. The other one in 2 Kings 14 is shorter but none the less pointed in its application. It is to be noted that both of these are tree fables. Of animal fables there is none in the Bible. In the Rabbinic literature, however, they are plentiful. Rabbi Meir was an adept at this kind of composition and tradition has it that he wrote 300 fox fables. In the time of Rabbi Johanan the references to only three of that number were extant.*[59] Jochanan Ben Zaccai a pupil of Hillel the great Halachic authority also composed fables.*[60]

Only one example of the riddle is to be found in the Bible. But from the example there given and from the circumstances there related, it is safe to assume that riddles were a common method of furnishing entertainment to guests assembled at feasts or weddings. (Judges 14, 14). The ḥidoth of the Queen of Sheba are not given in 1 Kings 19, 1=2 Ch 9, 1, but the later writings have not allowed the chance to go by without claiming to give some of them.*[61]

Of parables, and the parable is also included in the term mashal, there are a number of examples. One is pronounced by Nathan the prophet against David (2 Sam 12, 1-6) and through its lesson David is led to pass judgment upon his own actions. The second is given by a wise woman of Tekoa (2 Sam 14, 5-7). A third is found in 1 Kings 20, 39-40, the figure this time being drawn from military usages. A fourth, Isaiah 5, 1-6, is the parable of the vineyard and the disappointed hopes of the owner and lastly we have Isaiah 27, 24-28 also drawn from agricultural life. It is worthy of remark that of the five parables extant, three are drawn from agricultural conditions, the fourth from land inheritance customs, which touch therefore on the same general agricultural state as the first three, and the fifth is from war. The parable develops in later literature and becomes very frequent, when the pages of the Midrash have very often the opening sentence—"משל למה הדבר דומה."

But whereas the Biblical parable is, as already indicated, seen to be founded on the simplest circumstances of agricultural life and upon the early conditions which include the "Goel" conceptions, those of the Midrash are to a large extent products of and expressive of conditions as they were in the days of Roman suzerainty and supremacy. The parables there speak, therefore, of kings, of palaces, of landed proprietors, of retinues and imperial pomp. They know of the intrigue of palace, of favorite and of extensive building operations. (See for this Ziegler, Die Koenigsgleichnisse des Midrasch beleuchtet durch die Kaiserzeit, Breslau 1903.)

Besides meaning proverb, parable and fable, "mashal" is used in the Bible to indicate a sharp, jeering, taunting speech. The person thus addressed becomes in himself a "mashal"—an object lesson, a warning to others and a fitting subject for the moralists. "He hath made me a proverb among the people"—Job 17, 6. In this sense the speech directed by the prophet against Babylon is called a "Mashal"—Isaiah 14, 4ff. So Micah 2, 4 and Ezekiel 14, 8 where משל is used in combination with אות, Jeremiah 24, 9—here the combination is even stronger "a disgrace, a byword, and a curse," and Deut 28, 37 "Thou shalt become a desolation, a byword and a proverb among all the nations;" 1 Kings 9, 7—"And Israel shall become a byword and a proverb in all the nations;" 2 Ch 7, 20; Ps. 40, 5; 78, 2.

But the term "mashal" is applied also to poetic compositions without reference to proverb, maxim or gnomic saying at all. Thus for example, the speeches of Balaam are expressly called, each one, a mashal—Numbers 23, 7. 18: 24, 315. 20. 21. 23. In the same way the old selections concerning the destruction of Moab—Numbers 21, 27-30 are called mashal. Didactic Psalms are called mashal, Ps 78, 2.

The metaphor continued and developed passes over into the allegory, and this, too, is indicated by the term Mashal. Ezekiel 17, 3-10, 24, 3ff; Ps 80, 9-10 and many others.

So far the attempt has been made to gather the fragments of gnomic character, to show the extent of the proverbial literature of the Bible and for the sake of completeness to show the other forms of the mashal and the חדה even though only distantly related to our main preoccupation—the proverb. In the Apocrypha, we have naturally the book of Ben Sira, which is by far the largest book in the literature of proverbs. The Wisdom of Solomon cannot be included as a whole, for although it is a member of the wisdom class, its style is not such as would entitle it to be called gnomic. Chapters 10-19 are really an attempt to give an outline of the history of the Jewish people, particularly of the stay in Egypt and the deliverance from that land and to explain why the Egyptians were sent certain plagues. This section is in reality a sort of Greek Midrash. But even the first part cannot enter into the discussion and detailed analysis. For while it has reminiscences of Hebrew constructions the style, despite frequent parallelisms, is a Greek one.

Besides these two books, there are a few fragments that ought to be collected and mentioned. First is the fragment in Tobit 12, 6-11—an example of didactic gnomic literature with a particular person addressed, and not an assumed audience. The dependence of this passage on the canonical books is evident. Tobit 12, 6 "It is good to praise God and exalt his name and honorably to show forth the works of God" depends on Ps. 92, 2-3. Verse 7—"It is good to keep close the secret of the king, but it is honorable to reveal the works of God" has phraseology suggesting the vocabulary of Amos 3, 7 and Ps 25, 14. Verse 7b "Do that which is good and no evil shall touch you" is suggested by Psalm 91, 7.. Verse 8b "A little with righteousness is better than much with unrighteousness follows Ps 37, 16 and incidentally corroborates the emendation proposed of changing "hamon" into "hon" and suggests further Proverbs 15, 16. Verse 9—

"For alms doth deliver from death" is a copy of Proverbs 11, 14 besides giving the technical interpretation to "ẓedakah" of charity, and Ps. 79, 9. Tobit has another gnomic passage 4, 3-21, in its conception modelled upon frequent canonical usage—the patriarchs blessing their children, David blessing and charging Solomon. This passage in Tobit however insists far more upon the general religious and ethical principles than does the passage in 1 Kings 2. It becomes in this a forerunner of the extensive ante-mortem instructions as well as of the "ethical will" literature of the middle ages.*[62]

Baruch*[63] has a few verses on the praise of wisdom that ought to be classed with the gnomic—3, 29-35. Wisdom he there identifies with the Torah. The same dependence on the canonical books is here to be seen, though in general the style is a Greek style, particularly in the latter half of the book from Chapter 3, 9 on. Verses 29-30 are almost repetitions of Deut 3, 11-13 but what was said in Deuteronomy concerning the commandment of the Lord is here said about wisdom personified. "Who hath gone up into heaven and taken her, and brought her down from the clouds? Who hath gone over the sea, and found her and will bring her for pure gold?".

1 Esdras*[64] 3 has the account of the battle of the wits. In response to the query "What is the strongest thing in the world?" one answers "Wine," another "the King" and the third answers "Woman," and above all "Truth." The reasons for each answer are given in long gnomic passages—Chapters 3, 4—and the whole selection ends with a praise of truth.

1 Mac*[65] 2, 51-63 has another passage like this one in Tobith, the charge of the father to his sons. The contents of this, moreover, can be compared with a similar praise of the fathers, the section of the שבח אבות עולם in Ben Sira, Chapters 44-50. 2 Mac concludes with a comparison between

good wine and good speech somewhat gnomic in character; perhaps 2 Mac 2, 32 "It is a foolish thing to make a long prologue and to be short in the story" ought to be included as a proverb.

As has already been indicated, the proverb and the gnomic saying do not stop with the Bible and the Apocrypha, but continue straight on down through Jewish Literature. We have first to notice the Pirke Aboth—"The Chapters of the Fathers" of the Jewish Church*[66]. It is a part of the Mishnah although it has interpolations and additions of a later date, since the sayings of men are given who came some time after Rabbi Jehudah. The sixth Chapter is even later. The Aboth of Rabbi Nathan*[67] forms a sort of Gemara to the Pirke Aboth. Of Talmudic treatises Derech Eretz and Derech eretz Zuta contain proverbs. The number proverbs are collected in the Pirke Derabbenu Hakkadosh.*[68] The proverbs scattered throughout the Talmud have been collected in more or less complete form by various writers. Dukes, Blumenlese*[69] has good comparisons with the Midrashic and middle age literature but it cannot lay any claim to completeness. Schuhl "Sentences et Proverbes du Talmud et du Midrasch," Paris 1878, has comparisons with the classic authors. There is a book Millin Derabanan*[70] Perle, Sefer Ozar Leshon Ḥachamim, Warsaw 1900, has by far the most complete collection, though some of the quotations introduced can be called gnomic only by a very broad interpretation of the word. The Mibḥar Hapeninim*[71] comes into the literature through the Arabic. For other collections of the Middle Ages see Dukes Blumenlese, 54-56.

Not all the forms under the term mashal can properly enter into the discussion. It is evident that some fall far outside the subject. It is intended therefore to limit the discussion to the proverbs and maxims, and of the literature outside of the Bible and the Apocrypha it is proposed to make only use for the sake of comparison.

2. Form of the Gnomic Saying

Examination of the fragments as found in the historical and poetical books of the Bible will show that the proverbs were in many cases devoid of the parallelistic structure that characterizes the set proverb of the wisdom books. The proverb quoted as a "mashal ḳadmoni" in 1 Sam 24, 13 is a simple statement—מרשעים יצא רשע. The retort of 1 Kings 20, 11 is also of this simple nature—אל יתהלל חוגר כמפתח. Similarly void of the parallelistic structure is the quotation from popular theology in Jeremiah and Ezekiel concerning sin and heredity—אבות יאכלו בסר ושני הבנים תקהינה. Similarly 1 Sam 25, 25—כשמו כן הוא, and 1 Kings 12, 10—קטני עבה ממתני אבי and Habakuk 1, 14—כרמש לא מושל בו, Isaiah 22, 13—אכול ושתו כי מחר נמות; Ezekiel 16, 44—כאמה בתה, Judges 8, 21—כאיש גבורתו. That the completer form existed, 1 Sam 16, 7—כי האדם יראה לעינים ויהוה יראה ללבב ought to prove. The fragments in the prophets could not help being cast into the poetic mold, and therefore most of the proverbs found in the prophetic books have the parallelistic structure characteristic of the other portions of the writings. So Isaiah 28, 20; 66, 8; 49, 24; 45, 9-10; 40, 12-16; 33, 13-16; 32, 6-8; 10, 15; 1, 3; Jeremiah 49, 9; 18, 14; 17, 5-8; 9, 22-23; 8, 7; Amos 6, 12; 3, 6; 3, 5; 3, 4; 3, 3; Hosea 6, 3; 4, 14; (here from the context we have assumed that we have the b of a proverb of two members) 13, 3; 14, 10; 10, 12-13; 8, 7; 6, 6; 6, 4b. That the quotations in Ecclesiastes should have the parallelistic form is to be expected. The quotations in Psalms have the same structure as the work itself, therefore are parallelistic. With the aid of these fragments, then, the history of the proverb can be reconstructed. The proverb began as a simple statement, a pithy observation, and survived in such a form in later times either in the quotations from the mouth of the people, or as sayings whose proverbial force was recognized and therefore were allowed to stand as they were. But the poetical form of the rest of Hebrew writing seized upon the proverb and made it conform to the law of parallelism. When we get to the book of Proverbs, we have that structure highly developed, largely in the form of sentences composed of two members, that are compared affirmatively with each other with or without the sign of the connection, but often also antithetically placed. This structure of the Proverb exists outside of the wisdom books. As already pointed out, it is found also in the Prophets. Further it is found also in Ben Sira who modelled his style closely upon Proverbs. It is found moreover, in the gnomic fragments of the Genizah*[72] and of the three quotations of the still unidentified Eliezer Ben Irai, quoted by Saadia (see Harkawy, Zikkaron Larishonin pp 176, 178), one of which however is really a quotation from Ben Sira, two have this structure, one an antithetic parallelism and the other a comparison. At times when the relationship between the two members is that of comparison, it may not even be indicated, the two statements being placed side by side. Thus, for example, Proverbs 25, 11 תפחי זהב במשכיות כסף דבר דבר על אופניו "Apples of gold in figures of silver—a word spoken in proper manner." Compare with this Ben Sira 26, 18 which was most probably also put in this form—"Golden pillars upon sockets of silver—fair feet with a constant heart." The Greek version inserts "kai." Similarly Proverbs 25, 12 נזם זהב וחל כתם מוכיח חכם על אוזן שומעת "An earring of gold and a pendant of fine gold—a wise reprover to an ear that listeneth." Similarly Proverbs 25, 14 נשיאים ורוח וגשם אין איש מתהלל במתת שקר Clouds and wind without rain—a man that vaunteth falsely of a gift."

The distich grows into a tristich, common outside of Chapters 10-22 of Proverbs, for example, Pro 25, 8; 13, 20; 27, 10; 28, 10; or even into a tetrastich 26, 18.19. 24.25, and even a pentastich 25, 6-7. At times the proverb will grow to the length of proverbs 27, 23-27 or 24, 30-34.

A common form of the proverb in the fragments is the interrogative. Amos has it in 3, 4; 3, 3; 3, 5-6; 6, 12. Habakuk 3, 8. Jeremiah 18. 14; Isaiah 10, 15; 28, 24-25; 40, 12-16; 45, 9-10. 49, 15; 49, 24; 66, 8. Job has a number of such passages 6, 5-6; 7, 1; 8, 11. 12, 11. So has the Psalms—30, 10, 88, 11-13; 94, 9-10; 89, 49.

So far the inner structure. The sequence with which one proverb will follow another is, at least, in Proverbs, generally arbitrary. One proverb has slight or no connection with the next in thought. Some of the deviations in the text of the Septuagint are thus accounted for. Sometimes a catch word will suggest the following proverb. Perhaps it may be said that the subject matter will suggest the succeeding proverb without there being any strict logical connection. For example "king" suggests the order or better the placing of 16, 12-15 after verse 10. The notion of righteousness suggested the order of 11, 4-10.

If Bickell (Kritische Bearbeitung d. Proverbien W. Z. K. M. 1891) be correct, the letter of the alphabet suggested the order of some of the verses. Thus in Chapter 11, verses 9-12 begin with ב, in 20, 7-9 we have מ, in 20, 24-26 we have again מ, in 22-24 we have ע, in 22, 26-28 א, in 18, 20-22 מ once more, in 15, 12-14 ל. However, it is quite possible that this is purely accidental. One might as well argue that in the old alphabet the מ preceded the ל, because of a three-fold repetition of that order in 16, 17-18, 20-21, 22-23. If such a principle had obtained and had been consciously adopted by the compiler and carried out, we would expect to find more of it, and what is more important, in the face of the fact that alphabetic progression in composition was known we would be right in expecting in a conscious arrangement, which this theory implies, to see something more than a mere grouping of the same letters. We should see a progression in the alphabetic order. But nowheres under the conditions named is the next letter an advance in the alphabetic order upon the letter of the group. It is therefore necessary to assume that the succession of verses with the same initial letter is unconscious on the part of the compiler.

We do find proverbs alphabetically connected in Proverbs. (Pro 33, 10-31) and in the gnomic Psalms—37, where the alphabet is given in alternate verses. The ת is missing but it is easily restored by dropping the initial ו in 39. The ע can be restored by the suggested LXX reading (עולים לעולם בשמדו see Baethgen Com. in Loco). The alphabetic form is found also in Ps 25, 34, 111, 112, 119, 145. Ps. 34 misses the vav. Ps 25 begins with the aleph (the superscription, of course, can be omitted. In the second verse the beth can be taken from the בך. אלהי is by the Septuagint connected with verse 1, and while a transposition of the two words would still give the desired ב, the versions do not assume such a transposition. In Psalm 110, there are eight verses to each letter. Bickell had already forseen that Ben Sira 51 should be an alphabetic poem and attempted with this underlying thought a reconstruction according to the versions. By the discovery of the original Hebrew text, this restoration is, of course, set aside but his thesis is proven correct. The Alphabets of Sira*[73] will naturally suggest themselves but these are of late date—that is some of the proverbs are old but the alphabetic form and outline date from the tenth century and cannot therefore enter into the discussion here.

Besides the grouping of the proverbs under the alphabetic headings, there existed another method and in the discussion of this method the forms that we can find still lingering in the prophetic writings will be of great value. The form referred to is found in Pro 6, 16-19. The LXX has destroyed the form here by an ignorant misreading of both consonants and vowels of *shesh*, which it made over into *sas* and by misreading ושבע, into ישבר.*[74] The form is further found in Chapter 30 where statements are arranged under numerical headings—"two things have I asked of thee"—"four things are comely in their going" 29-31; four wise animals; four things the earth cannot bear 21-23; four things that are marvelous 18-20; four things that are insatiable 15-16; and seven things which are an abomination. Ps 62, 12 אחת דבר אלהים שתים זו שמעתי כי עוז לאלהים is cast into the mold of the number proverb but it is hardly to be considered a proverb. The same can be said of Job 33, 14—"For once doth the Lord speak and a second time and man will not see it" and of Job 40, 5—"One thing have I said and I shall not add." In Job 33, 29 הן כל אלה יפעל אל פעמים שלוש עם גבר there is the use of the numbers to indicate an indefinite quantity not at all parallel to the usage in Proverbs 30. The same use, to show indefinite number, underlies Isaiah 17, 6 שנים שלשה גרגרים, ארבעה חמשה 2 Kings 9, 32 שנים שלשה סריסים Micah 5, 4 שבעה רועים ושמנה נסיכי אדם Hosea 6, 2 יחיינו מיומים ביום השלישי יקימנו. The passages in Amos will be considered later.

To these there should be added the "two" proverbs which have by all commentators been neglected, but which, for a reason later to be given, ought to be included and especially noted—Proverbs 27, 3—"A stone hath heaviness and sand weight, but a fool's vexing is heavier than both" 29, 13—"The poor man and the man of exactions meet together, the Lord enlighteneth the eyes of both of them;" 24, 22————"who knoweth the ruin of both of them;" 20, 12—"The ear that heareth and the eye that seeth, the Lord hath made both of them;" 17, 15—"He who declareth the wicked innocent and he that condemneth the righteous, yea, both of them are equally abominable to the Lord." 20, 10—"Diverse weight and diverse measures are both of them an abomination unto the Lord." Ecclesiastes 4, 2-3—"Therefore praised I the dead, that are already dead more than the living that are still alive, and as happier than both of them, him who hath not yet come into being;" Ben Sira 40, 18-26, but for obvious reasons these are of secondary value since they may be consciously modelled on the form as found in Proverbs; Deut. 23, 19—"Thou shalt not bring the gift of a harlot and the price of a dog (male prostitute) into the house of the Lord for any vow. For both of these are abomination unto the Lord thy God." This last however, belongs here only because of the form. Proverbial value it has none.

The number proverb is found also in Ben Sira.*[75] There are three kinds of men that multiply sin and bring forth wrath 23, 16; in three things is wisdom beautified 25, 1; three sorts of men wisdom hates 25, 2; ten things wisdom judges happy 25, 7; four things wisdom feareth 26, 5; three things anger wisdom 26, 28; four kinds of vicissitudes that appear in man's life 37, 18; three nations that are abhorrent 50, 25-26.

It is important to note that many of these number proverbs are progressive: that is, they start with one number, make a statement and then add one more to the number and intensify the original assertion. Proverbs 30, 21 under three things the earth trembleth and four she cannot bear; 30, 15—there are three things that are never satisfied and four which will not say 'plenty'; 30, 29—there are three things which have a stately step and four which are comely in their going; 30, 18—there are three things which are too wonderful for me and four that I do not know. In Ben Sira, we have 26, 5—there be three things that grieve my heart and of the fourth I am sore afraid; 26, 28—there are two things that grieve my heart and the third makes me angry; 50, 25—two nations the heart abhorreth and the third is no people. The order "three and four" is the most common, occurring as it does five times.

But the number proverb has not reached its longest development in Proverbs and Ben Sira. It is found very frequently in later Hebrew literature. The fifth chapter of the "Chapter of the Fathers" contains many statements cast into this form, though some of them can hardly be called proverbial. In the number ten we have the "ten words of creation," the ten generations between Adam and Noah, and between Noah and Abraham, the ten trials of Abraham, the ten plagues. Of the number seven we have the seven qualities that characterize the wise man and the fool; the seven punishments meted out for seven specified sins. Of four, there are the four kinds of men classified by their attitude towards property rights, four kinds of minds, four kinds, or better, degrees of charity, four kinds of students. Of three, the three characteristics that mark the disciple of Abraham, and the three distinguishing the follower of Balaam. A collection of number proverbs seems to lie back of all of these. The section dealing with all this is not written in the general style of the Pirḳe Aboth which started out to be a record of the sayings of individual teachers. These are set down without regard to the authors, but are entered by numerical arrangement. A collection of number proverbs is to be found in the Pirḳe Derabbenu Haḳḳadosh (numbers 3 to 12). Dr. L. Grünhut in the Sefer Haliḳuṭim Jerusalem 1903. More are to be found in the שלשה ספרים נפתחים of Schönblum and in the third volume of the Beth Talmud, Vienna 1883.

A comparison of a number proverb running through the various sources will reveal a very interesting and important fact. The Pirḳe Derabbenu Haḳḳadosh (edition Schönblum) has under the number five (p. 18) the following proverb: חמשה אין הדעת סובלתן דל גאה ועשיר גזלן זקן מנאף ופרנס המתגאה

על הצבור בחנם והמגרש את אשתו שנים או שלשה פעמים ומחזירה:
"Five the mind cannot tolerate a poor man who is proud, a rich man who is a robber, an old man who is adulterous, the communal leader who lords it over the community and a man who divorces his wife two or three times and takes her back again."

It is quite evident that the proverb must have been originally concerned with the distinction between the rich and the poor and the qualities which are incongruous in each. Then out of the general notion of incongruity of actual quality and station with its supposed quality there arose the third. But the fifth member in this number proverb is assurredly out of place, while the fourth member no longer preserves the short concise statement into which the first three members are put. The fifth is even more clumsy in this respect. Now tracing the proverb backwards through the authorities, we find that in Tal. Bab. Pesachim 113b,*[76] the proverb is actually given as a number four proverb and the section that in the Schönblum edition makes it a proverb of five members is here given as a separate statement with the introduction formula "veyesh omerim" = "and some say." But the fourth member is clumsy and as seen does not correspond in style to the construction of the first three. A comparison with Sira 25, 2 shows that this awkward fourth was a later addition, and the proverb therefore appears as an original three-membered proverb. The one in Pesachim is evidently a quotation from Ben Sira, though no acknowledgment is there made of the source (the fact of the quotation is already noted by Reifman Haasif Vol 3). We cannot go further back and trace it to a two-numbered proverb. But this must have been its original form. Then it would have been thoroughly homogeneous. How the transition from a two-numbered proverb to one of the three class could be made is shown by the series in Ben Sira 40, 18-26 and in the similar forms given above in Proverbs,

Ecclesiastes and Deut. These have been by the commentators neglected, but in them we have the transition from the two to the three. In them the third member could be drawn from an entirely different sphere than the one to which the first two belonged as for example—"A child and a city establish a name, but finding wisdom is better than both" in Sira 40. Or this one in Proverbs—"A stone hath heaviness and sand hath weight, but a fool's vexing is heavier than both of them." The original form of the proverb in Sira would by this have been "A poor man who is proud and a rich man who is a robber are intolerable, but worse than both is an old man who is adulterous." That would satisfy all the demands of homogeneity of construction.

It is quite true that the number proverb is far more plentiful in later literature than in Proverbs and Sira. Nevertheless the contention that a proverb thrown into the number form is by that fact to be assumed of late origin as is generally assumed seems to me to be unwarranted. Wildeboer*[77] "Cap 30 und 31 gehören wahrscheinlich zu den jüngsten stücken. Darauf weisen die Zahlensprüche und das Alphabetische Lied am Schluss 30, 10-31." Frankenberg in his commentary*[78] to Proverbs 6, 16 has this to say concerning the number form—"Bereits in der ältesten prophetischen Literatur, bei Amos, auftretend, sind sie doch erst in der Spruchliteratur-Proverbien und Sirach—eine geläufige liter. Kunstgattung geworden." Toy*[79] referring to Pro 30, 11ff, says "the artificial tetradic form is probably late." He puts this section as late as 200 B. C. [See his article Proverbs in J. E.] "The fact that similar numerical proverbs were popular in the early Rabbinical period gives a certain support to the view that this collection is of late origin," see Cheyne, Job and Solomon p. 153, New York, 1887. But the one date, or better era, which is not in doubt, and about which criticism can give no other opinion, the time of the prophecy of Amos, makes it necessary for us to assume that the literary form of the number proverb must, contrary to the opinion of Toy, Frankenberg and Wildeboer and Cheyne antedate the reign of Hezekiah. Arguing therefore purely from the standpoint of form and that the number form, the collection of the number proverbs in Proverbs 30, instead of being exilic need not be later than the collection of the proverbs made by or under the direction of King Hezekiah. It must have been in existence much earlier. And for this reason. We have in Amos a usage of numbering which it is possible to assume, as Frankenberg does, is the origin of the number proverb and to explain as being an imperfect and rudimentary form of a later highly developed artistic one. Or it is possible to explain Amos, as does Nowack*[80] that "drei und vier dienen dazu eine unbestimmte vielheit zum Ausdruck zu bringen," or as Konig*[81] "wegen einer unbegrentzten und deshalb erschreckenden Reihe von Vergehen." But it is more to the point to say that Amos has his expression modelled after a current number system of proverb writing. Otherwise we could not understand Amos at all. His usage is quite different from the usage in Isaiah 17, 6 or 2 Kings 9, 32, Micah 5, 4 or Hosea 6, 2 above quoted. There the indefinite use of the numerals can be, and is, granted, and there the grammatical explanation will cover the case. But in Amos we have not a grammatical difficulty to explain or a question of lexicography to decide. His "for three transgressions———and for four" without the counting, or without any attempt at counting presupposes a mold which Amos had ready to hand. His phrase was dependant for its intelligibility and effectiveness upon the fact that the people were, through some source or another, acquainted with that numbered proverb form of expression and would in their minds pass over the three and dwell on the fourth which in the proverb style was the most weighty and important. Such a form is given to us in the proverbial literature in Pro., 30 and as has been shown above, the three-four proverb is the commonest form of the numbered-progressive proverb. That Amos wrote not without having literary models before him in his work is conceded. But these models have so far been limited to the literary productions of the prophetic classes. Harper*[82] speaks "of the prophetic technique and nomenclature which Amos found in existence." Davidson*[83] says—"In Amos, the oldest literary prophet, we find a religious nomenclature already complete." "Nothing is more clear than that he had predecessors in this work, who had developed in no small degree a technical nomenclature of prophecy." Harper*[84] says of Amos' materials—"Prophetic formulas which as employed by Amos show long and technical usage." But Amos had more than this. If the reasoning above given is valid, Amos had the proverbial technique as well. And this possession is substantiated by a further critical examination of the text of both Amos and Hosea. The quotations above given from the books of these prophets show that they had a popular proverbial literature and technique to draw from. Wildeboer*[85] speaking of the artistic forms of the proverbs, in an argument for the lateness says that popular proverbs "zeichnen sich gewöhnlich durch kürze und Einfachheit aus." But the fragments collected show that that period of beginnings must be put very far back. Hosea 4, 14b, in fact, presupposes a written document quoted by the prophet. The number proverb, therefore, instead of being late in the development of Hebrew literature is made by this study to date at least from the end of the ninth century. It demands that time be given for the spread of the knowledge of the form so that when Amos uses it in a skeleton outline, it would be recognized at once. At any rate the very latest limit for the dating of the appearance of the number proverb is fixed by the appearance of Amos as the heir to the literary, prophetic and proverbial craft of the earlier days.

So far we have made the attempt to establish the possibility of a numbered proverb text being comparatively old. The one argument that might at first militate against the assuming of Prov. 30 as possibly old is the presence of "Alḳum" in the numbered proverb in 30, 29-31 and of "Miẓ" in the section immediately following upon the genuinely numbered series. For while in section verse 23 there is no attempt at numbering we have here as well as in verses 11-14 virtually numbered proverbs. The argument then is, that these words being late testify that the sections in which they occur are late. We would set this argument aside, as being in the last analysis of very little or of no value. The question of vocabulary is of the least original decisive value in criticism. It is legitimately to be used only when it is employed as corroborative and contributory evidence. It cannot be legitimately used as starting point for an argument of dating, unless through other sources the dating has been established. Once a date has been fixed, then the study of the vocabulary is in order. It can never operate in the other direction. Of the least value moreover, as a help for dating is a word which is claimed to be Aramaic. The word confessedly Aramaic may have come late into the language, it is true. It may date, say from the Talmudic period for that matter. But on the other hand, it may be as early as the first wanderings of the early Hebraic Palestinian immigrants who came via many languages and especially through the language of the Syrian districts into "the land of the fathers." Ancient peoples also had international intercourse and many words were carried backwards and forwards along the lines of commercial relationship or of hostile and predatory incursions as well as in the border intermingling of blood. To seek to use Aramaic words as a means of dating without more ado is evidently impossible and may lead to absurd conclusions. It is no dating at all.*[86] Moreover, we have words in the so called later Hebrew that undoubtedly existed in earlier writings that were lost, or existed in the popular speech alone and were not called on to do duty in the written speech, because they were not needed. There was no occasion for them. As a matter of fact when we come to the popular proverbs, we do come across words that are found nowhere else. That is the case with "Maẓor" —"hindrance," 1 Sam 25, 14. Parosh "flea" occurs only in the popular saying 1 Sam 25, 14. Now it would be obviously inconclusive to draw deductions as to dating of the text or of the invasion of the flea in Palestinian households from this fact. It simply means that there was no occasion in literature of prophetic monition to mention the parosh, while popular speech preserved it. The "aluḳah of Chapter 31 Proverbs has the same history and interpretation. Maẓá owes its existence and survival in literature to the popular proverb in Isaiah 28, 20. And if the reading "mehithcanes" be maintained*[87] the Aramaism involved would be quite natural in a popular speech. "Masor" owes its survival to the proverb in Isaiah 10, 15. The word for little finger occurs only in the proverbs of 1 Kings 12, 10. Ḥabarburoth comes from the proverb in Jeremiah 13, 23. The root ḳahah is almost wholly a contribution of the popular proverb of Jeremiah and Ezekiel (31, 29 and 18, 2 respectively). It occurs elsewhere only in Ecclesiastes which approaches the conversational style and which for a reason to be given later, we consider in the same class with the popular proverbs of this type. The form helech "traveller," is found only in the parable in 2 Sam 12, 4. The very expressive figure "to extinguish the burning coal" meaning by that to destroy life is also a phrase of the popular proverb series (2 Sam 14, 7). The Stem LBT is found only in a quotation in Hosea and in a verse in Proverbs. It is following the same line of thought, and for the same reason that we have words in Proverbs that occur nowhere else. It is not a question primarily of dating or of time at all. And if there is nothing else to show dating the vocabulary solely should not be relied upon to establish it. It simply means that the book strikes a vein that others have not been called on to dig for. It implies that the proverb writer drew on an entirely different field of observation; other things came to his vision, than let us say, came to the writer of Leviticus, and therefore the vocabulary had to be different in a measure. So the "ant" "nemalah" is found only in Proverbs. Bearing in mind that we have in the Biblical Hebrew no word for the commonest things and operations for example, there is no word for "needle" in Biblical Hebrew, though it is found in so-called later Hebrew; that spinning was an ordinary operation, that the verb is found—"טוה" so is the word for the thing that is spun מטוה but there is no word for "spindle;" that there is no word for "loom;" that some of the words indicating tradesmen that are found in the Mishnah must be survivals of the old days, we can understand how much of a vocabulary existed without being registered in Biblical Literature. It is not surprising then that the popular fragments should have rescued a few from oblivion.

In short, the material at hand for the exact determination of dating through vocabulary is entirely too inadequate to give us the right to declare arbitrarily the line when the Biblical and the "late" meet and where the separation begins. As a matter of reason, much of what is called late Hebrew or marked in the lexicons as Neo-Hebrew or Mishnic with an implication of lateness of origin would really be found in early Hebrew—if we had the complete vocabulary of early days—though now is unfortunately only registered in the literature that we have in the late sources. It remains therefore, as previously stated that the number proverb is presupposed by the number formula of Amos and must have been developed long enough before his time to allow of its being used as he uses it, in outline, and the vocabulary argument is of no avail.

It still remains to show why, if the form of the number proverb is early, it was used so frequently in later times as to make it look like a late form of the proverb. This is to be accounted for by the following reasons. First, it is the simplest and most convenient way of adding to a proverb. When additions are made, instead of the shortest one dropping away, all of the lengths ran on in literature as separate and independent proverbs. This was shown when a proverb begins as a three numbered proverb in Sira and has a number added in a later source without the fact of the quotation being mentioned, without taking the original three numbered from the literature. Then a fifth number is added and we have three proverbs to take care of and tabulate instead of the last one only. Secondly, when literary style was no more marked by the rhythm and parallelism of Proverbs and Ben Sira and others under the spell of the Biblical writers, grouping was done in general by numbers. The alphabetic grouping was of course available. But by its very nature, it was available for longer extracts only. Grouping under the same letter is, as was stated above, contrary to the theory of Bickell,*[88] to be regarded as accidental. Besides alphabetic grouping demanded a certain amount of ingenuity and literary skill, and this was not always forthcoming. One of the most popular of books the Pirke Aboth, had a section of number statements. Now this book became very early a part of the liturgy. This brought it very close to the lives of the people. With this there came as a natural result a familiarity with the number formula. Lastly, what added still more to the growth of the number proverb was that the Halachah, for mnemonic reasons, has adopted the same plan of grouping (see Frankel, Darche Hamishnah, page 297, rule 40 note 2; also page 287, rule 28 and note). Under this guidance of Halachic grouping, the older number proverb degenerated into a jumble of things held together by the number. Thus the number proverbs in Aboth and to a greater degree even, the proverbs in Aboth of Rabbi Nathan became mere lexicographical lists. This very ease of composition brought about the decay of the number proverb.

In the hands of the unskilled in literary art, to whom henceforth it appealed, it degenerated into a bulky, unwieldy list of qualities, of men and things. It passed beyond the limits of literary art. Hence the gnomic fragments discovered by Schechter in the Genizah*[89] have not a single example of what was in former times the most popular mold for the Proverb. The Musar Haskel of Hai Gaon has but one example (Hai Gaon Edition Weiss p. 73). When it does appear in the literature of the middle ages, it can be traced directly to the Arabic influence. For this reason the Mibḥar Hapeninim abounds in the number proverb. (See Mibḥar Hapeninim ed. Dessau, Berlin 1842, pp. 6, 7, 9, 11, 13, 22, 25, etc.) For the number proverbs in Arabic Literature see Freytag Arabum Proverbia Vol. 3 pp. 56-63 for three-numbered proverbs; 64-65 eight-numbered proverbs; p. 65 two-numbered proverb; p. 76 an involved three-numbered; p. 343 two-numbered, also p. 347, 618 the three numbered proverb attributed to Abu-Bekr, also a four-numbered one p. 624, 608 and 609 proverbs attributed to Mohammed. At all events the root of the number proverb in Jewish literature extends into the pre-exilic period; it flourishes through the exilic and post exilic period until by its own weight it fell.

Of course, when the age of the completion of the Biblical canon was passed, a new element entered. How that new element will operate is best seen in Ben Sira, the Hebrew text of which we now have, to a large extent at hand. So strongly had the language and the turn of expression of the Bible imprinted themselves upon the people that he who would write, perforce, based his plans upon them. In the case of Sira it included the antithetic, the parallelistic and the rhythmic structure of Proverbs, e. g. ברכת אב תיסד שרש וקללת אם תנתש נטע "a father's blessing will give foundation to a root, but a mother's curse will pluck up the plant, 3, 9; or 6, 15 on the value of a friend—לאוהב אמונה אין מחיר ואין משקל לטובתו "Priceless is a faithful friend and his goodness is beyond weighing." Or this one on haste in prayer—אל תתקצר בתפלה ובצדקה אל תתעבר "Be not too short in prayer and do not neglect almsgiving."

Ben Sira makes one advance on Proverbs. He arranges his material under a system of thought progression—for example 3, 1-16, duties of children to parents and the rewards attendant upon the fulfillment of these duties—4, 1-10, duties to the poor—6, 5-17, on friendship, true and false—9, 1-9 conduct towards women, etc., etc. Naturally then, Sira will have longer proverbs than those ordinarily found in the canonical books. Here is one covering eight members (it is the one quoted by Saadia from the otherwise unknown Eliezer ben Iraai, Sefer Hgalui, p. 178, and that it was popular is attested by its being quoted frequently, see Schechter Jewish Quarterly Review Vol. 3 p. 690, 698-699 and attributed to Ben Sira in each case though with slight changes in the text). "Things too wonderful for thee search thou not. That which is hidden from thee seek thou not. Thou art not permitted to think thereon. Thou hast no concern with the secret things. Into that which is beyond thee intrude thou not, for thou hast been showed that which is too great for thee. For many are the thoughts of the sons of men, and wicked thoughts lead them astray." With the thought compare Ps. 131, 1, "O Lord, my heart is not lofty, neither are mine eyes exalted, and I have had no concern with the things too great and too wonderful for me" and Deut. 29, 28—"The secret things belong to the Lord our God, but the revealed things to ourselves and to our children," etc., and in the Mibḥar Hapeninim, Sha'ar Hayihud "They said to the wise man 'What is the creator?'

He answered, 'Speech concerning that of which it is impossible to have conception is folly, and discussion concerning that which thought cannot attain is sin'." There is a similar thought in Jehudah Hallevi ed. Harkawy, Vol 2, p. 106, "Search his ways and his deeds, but to Him do not stretch forth thy hand."

The influence of the diction of the Bible is very great upon Ben Sira. With him we have already the Paitanic style which grew so bulky and mechanical in later days. This Paitanic style takes from the Bible verses and parts of verses, sometimes uses them bodily without change, sometimes changes the form of the verb or makes some other slight modification in the expression, combines verses, and out of the mass makes a new composition. It can readily be seen that this practice is possible and of advantage only when the Bible and the Biblical turn of thought remained part of the most intimate intellectual possessions of both the writer and the reader. Its popularity would depend on the depth of knowledge of Biblical matters that the reader possessed and on his ability to understand hints and allusions to the canonical text. A splendid example of the style is to be found in the Maḥbereth Emanuel, pp. 44-50 in which every question is aptly answered by a quotation from the Bible. A few examples will show how far Ben Sira was influenced by the Bible text. It can be seen even in the English text by comparison of 2, 16 with 2 Sam 24, 14, but far more clearly in the Hebrew text. Beginning with the first few lines of the extant Hebrew text, we find that 3, 8b is founded on Deut 28, 2. There is some alteration in the form of and order of the words, but the expression is the same. So 3, 29b is founded on Pro. 2, 2. But is Daniel 4, 24 a quotation of Ben Sira 3, 30? Ben Sira 6, 6 is founded on Pro. 11, 4; 6, 14 ומוצאו מצא הון and reference to Proverbs 8, 35 shows what little change that is from מוצאו מצא חיים. Incidentally this proves the integrity of the Hebrew text as against the LXX "exodoi mou exodoi zoes." 6, 31 is based on Pro. 4, 9. There is no need to multiply examples—(see notes in the Wisdom of Ben Sira, Schechter and Taylor, pp. 13-25 on the text covered by the edition and also of Neubauer's text. For the remainedr of the text see Strack, Ben Sira and Smend, Wesiheit d, Jesus Sirach). The dependence however, is not completely indicated in any of the editions. Ben Sira well deserves the praise that his grandson, who translated the grandfather's Hebrew text into Greek, gives him. In speaking of the preparation that his grandfather brought to the work, he says, "My grandfather Jesus who had given himself to the study of the law, of the prophets, and other books of our fathers, and had gotten thereby good judgment, was drawn on also, himself to write something pertaining to learning and wisdom." To this indebtedness to those who went before him, and in whose footsteps he walked, a faithful follower, he himself confesses. "I awaked," he writes, "last of all, as one who gathereth after the grape gatherers. By the blessing of the Lord, I profitted and filled my vine press like a gatherer of grapes." 23, 16. His wide acquaintance with the Bible and the influence this acquaintance had upon his style is shown by the fact that he draws upon the historical, prophetic and poetical books alike.

Whenever 1 Mac departs from the narrative style and desires a poetic form to cover some song of praise or exhortation, it also falls into the Biblical style. See 1 Mac 1, 26-28: 39-40: 2, 7-13: 3, 3-8, 9: 2, 44; 3, 45; 7, 19 (17) "The flesh of thy saints have they cast out, and their blood have they shed around Jerusalem, and there was none to bury them" is an abbreviated quotation of Psalms 79, 2-3. 9, 20-21 where the Ḳinah measure seems to be preserved; 9, 41 and 14, 6-15.

That the Bible was not forgotten among gnomic writers in Israel after Ben Sira is amply proven by the unknown writer of the Genizah fragments above quoted. On page 5 line 14—page 6 line 1 we have an amplification of Jeremiah 9, 22, 23. The dependence of 9, 18 ושבת מריב יכבד upon כבוד לאיש שבת מריב Pro. 20, 3 is evident, and ותתענג כדשן נפשם is assuredly founded upon Isaiah 55, 2 ותתענג בדשן נפשכם. Compare the phrases in the two proverbs of this gnomic writer with the passage in Ps. 16, 11

דרשי חכמה מבקשי ד' יזכו בנעימות נצח
אוהבי בדעה דרך ה' ישבעון שמחות פני ה'

The author will even take up a difficulty in idiom—page 8 line 5 סוף דעת וחכמה יראת ה' כזה כל האדם from Ecclesiastes 12, 13. Here is a combination of Ps. 115, 5 and Isaiah 44, 8 עינים להם ולא יראו כי טח מהשכיל לבותם. But the acquaintance with the Scriptures does not prevent a neat turn and an excellent antithesis, on page 12 line 2 לב כסילים עיניהם ועין חכמים לבותם This might be compared with a similar turn in Sira 21, 26 "The heart of fools is in their mouth, but the mouth of the wise is in their heart." There might here be a dependence of the gnomic writer upon Ben Sira.

The attempt has been made to show that the proverb as it is found in the canonical books, devoted to wisdom literature, is but a section of a larger stream, currents of which are still to be found in the other books of the Bible; that the form of the proverb is the result of long work and literary effort, is built upon the foundation of a popular saying without the parallelistic mold, and gradually acquires the poetic form which is already completed by the time of the Proverbs, that this form is handed down through Ben Sira and to later writers, is lost in the writings of the Talmudic Literature and its allied branches but appears again in fragments; Saadia is witness to the fact that such books were written and to show their relationship to the Biblical books they were written or better, supplied with the marks of Biblical books; that the alphabetic proverb is found rarely in proverbs and just as rarely in Ben Sira (the Alphabet of Ben Sira being a much later work) hence as far as gnomic literature is concerned, the alphabetic form is found chiefly in the gnomic Psalms in the canon; that the number proverb dates from early times and must be assumed to antedate the earliest of the literary prophets, part of whose literary technique it must be assumed to have formed, or his style would not be explained; that this, from ease of composition and special adaptability to additions, and under the spell of the Halacha with its methodology and also under the promptings of the popular book of Pirke Aboth, became the most common form of the proverb, but because of its own weight, the form became non-literary and impossible from the literary standpoint, until from Arabic sources it regained some currency; finally that the style of Proverbs and the expressions of the Biblical books in general dominated and determined the form, the phraseology and the style of Ben Sira and the later gnomic writers.

3. Authors of the Gnomic Literature

Passages such as Proverbs 24, 23—"These also are the words of the wise men" and in the general introduction to Proverbs—Pro. 1, 6 "The words of the wise men and their dark sayings;" Pro. 22, 17—"Incline thine ears and hear the words of the wise men;" Sira 3, 24—"A wise heart will understand the proverbs of the wise men" (although it would not be conclusive, in the absence of other evidence, to deduce anything of this kind from Ben Sira because of the established fact that he copies Biblical phraseology and there his words do not carry the force of an original statement and wise *men* might in Ben Sira mean nothing more than wise *man*) point to the fact that in the gnomic literature we have to deal (besides with the few names that have been handed down to us in a more or less, usually less, recognizable shape) with a class.*[90] The honor in which the wise men were held as a class is shown by Ben Sira 38, 33, where after describing a number of occupations and summing up their values to the community he says, "Without these a city cannot be inhabited," but" these shall not be sought for in public counsel, nor sit high in the congregation, they shall not sit in the judge's seat, nor understand the sentence of judgment, they cannot declare judgment and they shall not be found where parables are spoken." The same high praise is expressed in almost identical phrases and divisions in Jeremiah 18, 18—"For the law will not be lost from the priest, nor counsel from the wise, nor the word from the prophet." Ezekiel 7, 26 has the same division, "But they will seek vision from the prophet, and the law shall be lost from the priest and counsel from the elders." It is to be noted that for the "ḥachamim" of Jeremiah we find the "Zeḳenim" in Ezekiel. Such a parallel with a difference is full of significance. The "Ḥacham" is placed in some relationship with the judge and the lawgiver. This relationship while in Comparative Semitics is recognized at the roots, is usually overlooked later on. This has led to difficulties when they might have been easily avoided. Deuteronomy 16, 19 is a case in point. כי השחד יעור עיני חכמים ויסלף דברי צדיקים. The Ḥacham in this case is surely none else than the judge. צדיק is to be taken in the same sense. It does not deal with the person to be judged. This interpretation of צדיק as the "just" as indeed it is usually interpreted does not harmonize with the general intent of the passage, which aims at insuring justice by preserving the incorruptibility of the judges. It therefore describes the effect of bribery upon the judges. Therefore the צדיק or the חכם is the righteous judge. What he gives is variously indicated as חכמה or משפט. See Ps. 37, 30 פי צדיק יהגה חכמה ולשונו תדבר משפט Proverbs 21, 15 can be interpreted only in this way. Toy*[91] makes it mean—"The execution of justice is a joy to the righteous, but the destruction to the evil man." But bribery was the immediately preceding thought. It ought to be understood as—"It is a joy to the righteous to do justice and to bring destruction upon those who work evil." Jeremiah has the sense of the administration of justice involved—"Behold days are coming, saith the Lord, and I shall raise unto David a righteous sprout, he shall reign, and he shall prosper, he will do justice and righteousness in the land," Jer. 23, 5. That צדיק is used in the legal sense is of course nothing new but then it is by the commentators limited to the litigants—as in 1 Kings 8, 32 "Thou in heaven wilt hear and thou wilt do judgment, and thou wilt judge thy servant to condemn the guilty and to put the evil of his way upon his head and to acquit the *innocent* (ולהצדיק צדיק is the Hebrew) and give him according to his righteousness."

But in a passage as Zephaniah 3, 5, it is hard to maintain the passive meaning of "the right." Nowack*[92] misses the force of the passage when he renders it "Jahve ist gerecht in ihrer Mitte." I propose the rendering in line with the argument above—"The Lord is judge in her midst, he will not do iniquity, morning after morning doth he bring his justice to the light of day." Further, in Zephaniah 3, 3-4 we have the divisions of three classes as we had them in Ezekiel and Jeremiah, but in the place of the חכמים of the one and זקנים of the other Zephaniah has a substitution full of significance, of the שפטים. Proverbs 29, 2 should be considered in this connection. ברבות צדיקים ישמח העם, ובמשל רשע יאנח עם The LXX reading*[93] here is a divergent one. In the first place it must have had the plural instead of the singular Ha'am. That however, is inconsequential. The rendering of the first two words is according to them "when the righteous are praised." But that destroys the parallelism. Toy*[94] emends into "birdoth" when the righteous rule. But the integrity of the reading "birvoth" is maintained by the reading in Pro. 29, 16 ברבות רשעים and by the use of the root in the sense of "govern" in Proverbs 28, 28. The verse ought to be rendered as follows: "When righteous judges rule, the people rejoice, but when the wicked judge rules, the people sigh." That רשע is used in this sense of wicked judge, a judge amenable to bribe taking, is clear from the passage in Proverbs 17, 23 which verifies at the same time the use of צדיק as judge of course with the implication a righteous judge—"The wicked judge will take a bribe from the bosom to pervert the ways of justice" שחד מחק רשע יקח להטות ארחות משפט. So, to return to Exodus 23, 8 and Deuteronomy 16, 19, we have in both members of the verse a legal terminology involved, but completely concerned with the judge and not with the litigants. The חכם and the צדיק are thus to be taken in the sense of "judge." Besides, the use of חכם in this sense is warranted by Jeremiah

50, 35—"A sword over the Chaldeans saith the Lord, and to the inhabitants of Babylon, to its rulers and to its 'wise'." In Jeremiah 51, 57 the ḥacham is placed in a long list of the officers, rulers and governors. The judge idea is present in the Arabic, but finds only these few traces in the Hebrew. Later Hebrew of course makes use of the word to mark the learned man, learned in the law, and thus through the identification of the Torah with Ḥochmah, the original meaning of ḥacham is restored. Following this suggestion, ḥochmah is first of all the utterance of a judge, a judgment in other words. Gradually it came to be used in the wider sense exactly as it has been developed in English where judgment indicates besides the judicial notion, a clean, clear cut statement on the issues of life made by a man of experience and wisdom. The parallelism that existed between the Ḥacahmim and the zeḳenim (compare the passages above quoted, and then with the shofeṭim) implies the same history. They were, therefore, the men who were taught by experience, and because of this knowledge gained in the school of life, they gained authority among the people. Taught by life, they gave their wisdom to others who would live wisely. This is the attitude throughout in Proverbs. It is the kindly guiding hand of the old leading the young, holding them as a father would his son, addressing them as such, warning them of the pitfalls, dangers and temptations. That is the attitude seen also in the gnomic Psalms (32, 8-9; 34; 94, 8 and elsewhere). If the priest taught from ceremonial law, and the prophet from the direct preachment of his "Word" or "Burden" or "Vision," the wise man was satisfied to preach from his own homely experience. See for this Proverbs 24, 30-34 and Job 5, 2ff. His philosophy was practical philosophy. His school was life. His reward was a certain practical success in life's endeavors. "Do not forsake the talk of the wise men and in their sayings spread thyself, for from them wilt thou gain instruction to stand before rulers" advises Ben Sira 8, 8-9. "Do not disdain to hear from the elders that which they heard from their fathers, for from them wilt thou gain the understanding to make the proper answer when it is needed." It is conceivable that the wise man should have been able to reach some of the people whom the others, priest and prophet, could not reach. That the method of the wise man, frequently with the personal element strongly expressed, was a popular one is shown by the fact of the imitation of his style by the Psalmist Ps. 37. That the wise men were not opposed to the prophet it is hardly necessary to say. The Genizah fragments have this verse*[95] לב נבונים כלב נביאים כי בתורת נביאים תמוכים. The Talmud is even more generous in its praise of the wise men. See Talmud Babli Baba Bathra 12a.*[96] What the prophets thought of the wise men has been shown above. The wise men are equally generous in their praise of Prophecy. "When there is no vision, then do the people become unruly"—Proverbs 29, 18. This much is certain, Sira studied his prophets assiduously, and even if he had not said it, his language would have betrayed it. The other class, the priestly class, inasfar as it was the representative of the sacrificial system, was outside the ken of the wise men. Still the wise men did not condemn sacrifice. The most that they would say is that obedience is better than sacrifice. Proverbs 21, 3—"The doing of justice is preferrable to sacrifice." The other passages quoted by Cheyne*[97] Proverbs 15, 8; 21, 27; 16, 6 cannot be made to state even this comparison between righteousness and sacrifice. All they state is that sacrifices cannot be used to cover up iniquity. This attitude was not peculiar, however to the gnomic school. We find similar statements in the prophets—Hosea 6, 6; Micah 6, 7-8; Amos 5, 24; and 1 Sam 15, 22. The enthusiastic love of the priest that Ben Sira has is well brought out in his section on the "Praise of the Fathers" when he speaks of the ceremonial system and the sacrifices. See also Ben Sira 7, 29-31—בכל לבך פחד אל ואת כהניו הקדיש בכל מאודך אהוב עושך ואת משרתיו לא תעזוב כבד אל והדר כהן ותן חלקם כאשר צוותה. This position is in harmony with the prophetic school and would only disagree with a distorted and mercenary priestly system. Other complaints can be brought against it, and the prophets and the gnomic writers are not silent on this, but it is not necessary that the priestly system, was iniquitous per se. At time such an iniquitous state of affairs did exist among some of the priests, the priesthood was bought and sold, but then it was due to wrong doing on the part of the individual. The wise men would not lay the blame upon the priestly idea.

That the historical backgound to the proverbial literature is to be enlarged was clear from the passages in Amos, where the deduction was made that we must assume a finished form of the proverb including the technique of the number proverb before the time of the earliest of the literary prophets, or else the form of Amos could not be understood. This was made even clearer by the fact that in Hosea and Amos we have the remnants of Proverbs. Hosea quotes what seems to be the second half of a proverb.[*08] The historical background must be enlarged in one more particular. The other classes with whom we had to deal and with whom the wise men are frequently mentioned had their false counterparts. There were the prophets of the Lord, the true prophets, and there were the prophets of falsehood. There were the priests of the Lord and there were the priests of the various forms of worship antagonistic to the Jahveh worship. See on this particularly the extended attack on the false prophets in Jeremiah 23. The misreading of Isaiah 28, 14 and of Proverbs 29, 8 but more particularly of the Isaiah passage, is responsible for the fact that a whole series of sayings has not been put in proper light. Isaiah uses the term "Moshele ha'am" in the text evidently to indicate a counterpart of the "Ḥacham" just as the "neviai hasheḳer" are the counterparts of the "neviai Jahve. By "anshe laẓon" he understands the phrase makers. There is therefore a school of the real wise men, with the Mishle Ḥachamim (see Hebrew text of Ben Sira 3, 29) and a school of the false wise men. These latter are the moshele ha'am. It is to be assumed from the nature of the case that the false wise men would ally themselves naturally with the false priests and the false prophets; they are therefore mentioned in conjunction with them by Isaiah. It is natural too, that in the victory of the prophetic school, all literature antagonistic to that school should have been suppressed. Whatever of the literature of these moshele ha'am remains, exists only in fragments. They are found only when quoted by the prophets and by them combatted. But the fragments are numerous enough to make it worth while to collect them. Koheleth can be looked on as the largest fragment of the Moshele ha'am school to which a ḥacham unable to give longer answer simply added the ending—"as long as all is in doubt, the best thing is to come back to the fear of the Lord. This is the end of all things." It is on this theory that we can explain the later fortunes of the book. It was not granted ready admission into the canon. Unconsciously there lingered in many minds some reminiscence as to its heretical origin. For this reason while its conclusion, the work of a ḥacham was satisfactory and actually procured its admission into the canon, the book was felt to be out of alignment with the rest of the literature. The sign of holiness, making the hands impure, ritually, was not given to it without discussion.*[99] During the same period of questioning and examination for admission into the canon, two other books—Ben Laana and Ben Tagla were kept out.*[100]

Furthermore, this contention against the uniform and arbitrary rendering of "anshe laẓon" by "men of scorn" will be supported by the examination of the passages in which words of this root accur. This examination, moreover, will place leẓ in the proper light as well. It begins with the sense of making phrases, that is in the good sense, then as frequently happens (just as rhetorician was used in the good and bad sense and as sophist was a term of blame only later) the leẓ becomes the adherent of the popular philosophy, the theologian and the unwise wise man. From that he easily passes over into the company of the wicked. That we have the intermediate step, the popular phrase maker, rather than scoffer and scorner, has been overlooked.

Laẓon itself occurs three times. Pro. 1, 22—"How long, ye simpletons, will ye love folly and ye leẓim love laẓon and ye fools hate wisdom." It is hard not to see that the leẓ and his love, laẓon, found in the company of the simpleton and the fool is the man who has a perverted ḥochmah. Therefore is he the one frequently addressed by Ḥochmah Proverbs 29, 8 "Men of false wisdom overturn a city, but the wise men turn away wrath" has the opposition again between the false popular wisdom and the real wisdom strongly expressed. In the passage in Isaiah 28, 14 the same opposition is expressed. The prophet had spoken. From his answer to the anshe laẓon it is to be judged that his prophecy was cast into short phrases which the popular phrase makers took up. They therefore speak of "ẓav laẓav and ḳav laḳav." To this they added their own phrase about their security. On this Isaiah tells them to stop this phrase making. This is the interpretation to be put on "Al titloẓaẓu." It does not mean "do not scorn." It is almost technical in force. "Do not continue making phrases as you have been doing about your security, etc. Make no more of your proverbs, but hear the real teaching." He ends the chapter then with a gnomic passage which in this interpretation becomes an integral part of the prophecy. The style of the section 28, 23-29 is of course different from the rest of the chapter. It cannot help but be different. It is intentionally put into the Ḥochma style to teach the Anshe laẓon the folly of their wisdom. So far laẓon has not been found in the sense of scorn. That rendering gives a faulty and inadequate understanding of the case in all three passages.

The verb is used in a good sense in many of the passages. So Meliẓ is an interpreter—a neutral sense, at least, in 2Ch 32, 31; Isaiah 43, 27; Genesis 42, 43. The use in Job 33, 23 is a decidedly good use of the word. In Proverbs 9, 12 in a rather connected extract, for wisdom is there represented as addressing her audience, we have אם חכמת חכמת לך ולצת לבדך תשא Frankenberg*[101] renders—"Wenn du weise bist, bist du's dir zu Nutze, and wenn du ein Spotter bist, hast du's allein zu tragen." Toy*[102] has—"If thou art wise thou art wise for thyself, and if thou art a scoffer thou alone must bear the consequences." Wildeboer*[103] translates—"Bist du ein Spotter." Now the context must be taken into consideration in this passage. We have here a picture in two sections. Wisdom personified speaks, and tries to influence her hearers. Folly, too, is personified. In verse 12 (whether 7-12 belongs originally to Ḥochmah and is a part of her address or was later slipped in or a transition is immaterial to the argument*[104]) we have the statement on the part of wisdom or on the part of the interpolator, that the choice must be made and the consequences, good or bad, come naturally. But the choice lies between wisdom and laẓon. There is here exactly the same opposition that there was in Isaiah 28, 14ff. The other passages in which the verb is used can be allowed to stand as "scorn" passages. These are Proverbs 14, 9; 19, 28; 3, 34; Ps. 119, 51; Hosea 7, 5; the verse in Job 16, 20 is doubtful but it is most likely used in a bad sense of the word—"My friends have misunderstood (misinterpreted) me" therefore Job turns to God.

The word leẓ is found in the company of the kesil and the pethi as already noted in Proverbs 1, 22. The same companionship is given him in Pro. 19, 25 as also in 21, 11. In these proverbs the leẓ is the man who has turned from the real wisdom of the wise and has found something else for himself, which he, indeed, calls and thinks wisdom, but which will speedily prove itself unreliable and worthless. Therefore the special invitation comes to him to come and learn the real wisdom Pro. 1, 22. Isaiah has an important passage, important for the understanding of the real position and character of the leẓ. Beginning at chapter 29, verse 9 and interpreting in accordance with the interpretation that we have given 28, 14, we have the picture of the delusion of the people. The prophet calls them drunk but not with wine. They have been misguided. The day will come when the wisdom of the wise men will be brought to naught. Then will true wisdom come to its own. Ariẓ (29, 20) is here used not in the sense of the tyrant but in the sense in which we find it in the gnomic literature as a parallel to the wicked man. See Job 15, 20; 27, 13. The wise men are blamed for their utterances and upon examination these are seen to be of the same character as those attributed to the Moshele ha'am and the anshe laẓon in Isaiah 28, 14. The leẓ is in Isaiah 29, 20 the singular of anshe laẓon. In this interpretation the מחטיאי אדם בדבר so vexing to the commentators*[105] becomes clear. They have misled the people by their sayings.

Yayin personified as a teacher and called a leẓ is another such proof. The fantasies of the drunk bear the same relationship to the calm reasoning of the sober, as this false wisdom bears to the real wisdom. Other passages can be allowed to stand as they are. They are entered here for the sake of completeness—Pro. 22, 10; 21, 24; 19, 29; 3, 34; 9, 7; 13, 1; 15, 12; 14, 6.

Meliẓah is in both of the cases where it occurs used in the technical meaning. In Proverbs 1, 6 it is used as something well classed with wisdom, the mashal, the ḥidah, etc. The LXX it is true renders it by "skoteinon logon" (edition Swete) but that is hardly correct. The rendering is caused by the propinquity of meliẓah to ḥidoth in the text. In Habakuk 2, 6 it is used for a taunting speech, exactly as mashal was used. Now it is hard to assume such a technical meaning in one part of the root, in meliẓah and then not find it in other words of the same root. As a matter of fact, by our assumption, we have found in all of the words of the root the same technical indication. When used technically it is in the sense of the false wisdom, the empty phrase maker, the opponent of the wise man, the popular theology as against the real religious doctrine. That opens up a whole field of possibilities but unfortunately, the literature owing to its very nature it was doomed, in the ascendency of the prophetic school, to destruction, and such indications as are found, are found in hints and in fragments.

It is fortunate, therefore, that a number of the prophets make it their practice to sum up for contradiction, or for the same purpose actually give, the saying of the popular phrase makers. Introduced by האומרים or אמרו or by some other such indication, we have a short chapter of the sayings of the false wise men. Such quotations from the heretical literature of the day, or if that is too strong, from the heretics of the day are as follows:

First of all would be the phrase quoted both by Ezekiel and Jeremiah—"The fathers have eaten sour grapes and the teeth of the children stand on edge." That, it seems, was a stock phrase of the heretical wise men. The force of this proverb acted both ways. That the other side of the proverb was not quoted here is supplied by the long argument that Ezekiel feels called upon to make proving or at least contending that the children of the righteous cannot live by the righteousness of the parents. When put objectively this will remind of the principal theory that the prophets had to combat. The temple is there. God must be with his people therefore. No danger can as a consequence do more than threaten. That is one of the האומרים in Amos 9, 10—"By the sword shall die all those sinners of my people who say 'the evil cannot approach and come to us'." If Ezekiel 11, 3 is interpreted to mean that the people said they were safe, even as the pot protects the flesh in it from the flames then we have another passage of similar intent there. So also Micah 3, 11—"Its chiefs judge for a bribe, its priests teach for a price, and her prophets divine for silver, and still they lean on God and say 'Is not God in our midst, evil cannot come to us'." On this thought the classic example is Jeremiah 7, 4. אל תבטחו לכם אל דברי השקר לאמור היכל יהוה היכל יהוה היכל יהוה המה. Giesebrecht*[106] takes the המה in the plural because the writer cannot help but think of משכנות יהוה in the plural. But it looks as if the המה should be construed with a "sheker" left out because of the "sheker" earlier in the sentence. The omission is of course older than the LXX. Jeremiah says "Temple of the Lord, Temple of the Lord, Temple of the Lord"—"They (the prophets) are false."*[107] Giesebrecht's interpretation would be a clumsy way of saying the temple stands. In the Moshele Ha'am verse Isaiah 28, 14 we have an amplified form of the popular mashal. It is here to be supposed that Isaiah continues their saying and carries it out to an absurdity. "Ye have said 'we have made a covenant with death and with Sheol have we made an agreement. The storm, when it passes shall not come to us, for (and this is the prophet's addition) we have made lying our refuge and in falsehood shall we find shelter'." Ezekiel 12, 22 has another quotation from the heretical literature—"The days are passing and the prophecy is failing," given by Ezekiel because he answers it in the counter proverb. Another such remnant is found in Isaiah 9, 9—"Bricks fall, we shall build of hewn stone, sycamore trees are cut down, we shall put cedars in their place." Haggai 1, 2—"The people have said 'The time has not come—the time for the temple of the Lord to be rebuilt." The LXX*[108] leaves out the first "time." That makes smoother reading, but is hardly necessary. The necessity of answering popular proverbs influences Malachi to such an extent, that it becomes a characteristic of his style. (1, 2; 1, 7; 1, 12; 3, 7; 3, 8; 3, 13-14.)

It still remains to be said that women took part in the development of the gnomic literature. From one of the authorities in Proverbs we have the direct statement that his mother taught him what he was about to utter (31, 1). The phrase אשר יסרתו אמו means more than the ordinary statement "the instruction of the mother" which in such case means the instruction in the art of living and not in the art of writing proverbs, which here, however, it undoubtedly means. That women practiced the composition of parables and the like, we know from 2 Sam 20, 18; 14, 6-7.

At the head of the whole school, not however in time, stands Solomon. Psalmody looks back in similar fashion to David. This was merely a matter of accepted tradition. By the same authority of tradition eschatology groups itself around Enoch. While Ben Sira is explicit in his praise of Solomon (47, 17) בשיר משל. חדה ומליצה עמים הסערת the Midrash seeks to establish a parallel between Solomon and David.*[109] "David composed proverbs, so did Solomon." To reward Solomon for the loss of his title to sole proverb writer the Midrash as does the Bible makes him as well as David, a writer of Psalms. The passage in the Bible concerning the Solomonic authorship of proverbs, reads as follows (1 Kings 5, 12ff) "And he spoke three thousand proverbs concerning the trees from the cedar that is in the Lebanon even the hyssop that springeth up out of the wall. He spoke concerning the beasts and concerning the creeping things and concerning the fishes." It is fair to assume that even in the mind of the recorder of this tradition, the proverbs, here referred to, if indeed a reference is made to Proverbs, were spoken and not written down. How this kind of a tradition could be amplified is readily seen from the Haggadic legend that Solomon spoke TO*[122] all the creatures and not OF. This form of the tradition passed over into other literatures.*[110] The text of 1 Kings above quoted however, does not give more than a vague statement of Solomon's wisdom and cannot be made to cover the Book of Proverbs, even by the most liberal interpretation. The אזוב hyssop is not even mentioned in the Book of Proverbs. Neither, strange to say, is the ארז cedar. The others in this list of the extent of Solomon's reach are less definite but the words דג and רמש do not occur in the book. It cannot be assumed therefore that the man was giving a brief summary of the book, when he mentions things that do not occur there at all. With direct reference to the Book of Proverbs eliminated, what can the passage mean? Nothing more than a rather extended acquaintance with trees, the habits of animals and the like and the knowledge was as far as we know only spoken and never written down.*[111]

By its own records, Proverbs has different layers. There is the collection of the sayings of Solomon made in the time of Hezekiah. Besides this we know from its own confession other compositions not of Solomonic authorship were added to the collection. Chapter 24, 33 we read גם אלה לחכמים "These also are the sayings of the wise men." The "also" points back to 22, 17-24, a section characterized by the direct address from the speaker to the listener. Then we have by the same testimony, Chapters 30 and 31 writings of Agur the son of Yakeh and Lemuel respectively. How far the authorship of Chapter 30 is to be attributed to one author is not clear. It is possible that the number section is a distinct section. Both of the names are in the Haggadic

Literature taken as disguises for Solomon himself. This is in line with the tradition of assigning all of the literature of proverbial character to Solomon. The same is done in the case of Koheleth, though there the reference to the fact that the author speaks of himself as being king in Jerusalem led to the identification. The interpretations of the Haggadah, however, were in all these cases, for homiletic purposes.*[112] Modern guesses have not gone beyond the conjectural stage. There is not enough material for decision in any case and Agur and Lemuel remain unsolved and unidentified.

Of the other book in the proverbial literature, we have a continuous biography. Written in Hebrew, by Simon the son of Jesus, son of Eliezer, son of Sira (so the name is given in the Hebrew text 50.27a and in 51, 30 (3) although 51, 30 (2) has Simon the son of Jesus called Ben Sira. In like form is the name given in Saadia's Sefer Hagalui, ed. Harkawy p. 150, line 10-11, but simply Ben Sira p. 162, line 7, and Bar Sira 162, line 18 and page 176, line 16 in both of which cases Harkawy makes the note that without doubt this is a mistake of the scribe for Jesus the son of Sira) it was translated into Greek by his grandson who came to Egypt in the 39th year of the reign of Euergetes, and since only the second of that name reigned that long (170-116 B. C.) he must have come to Egypt in 132 B. C. This date helps us moreover to identify the Simon of whom Ben Sira speaks so enthusiastically in his praise of the Fathers. There were two of that name but it can only be the second to whom Ben Sira refers. Ben Sira flourished therefore about 190-170. The Hebrew text was in time lost, though snatches of it are preserved in current literature, in the Talmud.*[113] Saadia (Sefer Hagalui, edition Harkawy) has seven quotations and an eighth one which he wrongly ascribes to another, an otherwise unknown author, Eliezer be Irai, the author of a book which he describes as being similar to the Book of Ecclesiastes ספר חכמה הדומה לספר קהלת What the style of the book was, is in one particular given us. Saadia says it was provided with the marks and the characters of the Biblical books. It must have been another one of the gnomic literature modelled closely upon Biblical models. The few quotations of the book verify this. In 1896 the first fragment of the Hebrew text of Ben Sira was identified and through additions from various sources a goodly portion of the Hebrew text of Ben Sira has been brought to the light of day.

Sira comes closer to his hearers, or better to his readers, than any of the writers of the Bible or the Apocrypha, with the possible exception of the sorrowing Jeremiah. Sira was born in Jerusalem (Ben Sira 50, 27). The accusation before the king, 51, 6 (Greek version*[114] *βασιλεῖ διαβολὴ γλώσσης ἀδίκου* does not materialize in the Hebrew text. Thus the political troubles are removed. He travelled in the pursuit of wisdom 34, 11. It may be that on such travels, he came across men of the Greek thought and particularly of the Stoic school. It is therefore quite likely that the verse referring to the five senses is genuine. That the Greek does not have it does not brand it as spurious. 16, 16 is also held spurious, for a similar reason, but a corruption *τω αδαμαντι* can only be understood if we presuppose an original Hebrew reading "livnai adam" which the translator misread very ignorantly as Avnai odem—hence "stones of adamant." For another notice of the five senses see Gnomic fragments of the Genizah (Jewish Quarterly Review, vol. 16, pp. 425-442) page 6, line 15 ff. "The light of the eyes and the hearing of the ears, the smell of the nose and feeling of the hands, the tasting of the palate and walking of the feet; all of these are given to all the living things, but above all of these is the speech of the lips, that is found only in man."*[115] On his travels too he seems to have made the acquaintance of the Greek banquet. Of this he learned to speak with favor and he takes the opportunity to praise it very frequently. Nor was he overanxious that the banquet should be marked by heavy and pedantic talk. In friendly fashion, he tells the old man who is to sit at the head of the table to "be one of the boys." Sira however, knew the canon too well not to emphasize the dangers of too much wine (Proverbs passim, Hosea 4, 11. Isaiah 5, 11. 21. See also gnomic fragment of Genizah "Wine enters, sense departs." Compare this with the later proverb of Tanḥuma, Shemini, "Nichnas yayin yaṣa sod." A quality of Ben Sira, which ought to be noted is his pride in his people's history. He uses it for illustrative purposes more than any other writer. In this he has placed himself in debt to the gnomic Psalmist. These showed him how to write history pragmatically, a quality handed on likewise to the wisdom of Solomon. Ben Sira glories in the "Law." His delight is in its study. The highest praise is given to the scribe of the Law. These are indication of the early rise of the Talmudic spirit—of the study of the law for the sake of the law.

Here ought to be added a notice of two other names that are mentioned in close association with the early gnomic literature—early in the sense that they belong somewheres soon before the completion of the canon. In the discussion of the "Sefarim Ḥiẓonim," the book of Ben Tagla and the book of Ben Laana are mentioned in connection with Ben Sira. There are no quotations extant from either book, so the contents are mere conjecture.*[116]

4. Sources

Following in the main tne outline mapped out by Koenig (Stilistik, Rhetorik Poetik, Leipzig 1900, pp. 83-84) but adding the material gained from the study of the fragments, the following are the chief sources whence the material of the gnomic lietrature is drawn. Koenig traces some of the proverbs to the world of minerals, e.g. Sira 23, 14-15 "What is heavier than lead, sand and salt and a mass of iron is harder to bear with than a man without understanding." Many of the examples which he enters in this class are only secondarily appropriate here. They should be entered in a class by themselves under the heading of the arts, coming properly therefore as a subdivision of the section man, or the fourth division in his system. In the class of the inanimate nature, Koenig fails to count the nature source which is abundant in the fragments. Natural phenomena are frequently drawn on by the fragments in the prophets. Hosea 6, 4b "and your kindness is as the cloud of the morning and as the dew which disappears in the morning." Hosea 6, 3 also draws on the same source. Hosea 8, 7 "They sow the wind and reap a whirlwind." Hosea 10, 13 "Ye have plowed evil, wickedness shall ye reap." See for this also Ps 7, 15. Hosea 13, 3 has as sources the natural phenomena of cloud, dew, chaff driven before the wind and smoke. Note also in the proverb in Job 5, 6. "For iniquity rises not from the ground and from the earth wrong doth not spring up." Job 14, 6-10 not altogether wholly gnomic is near enough. It too has the natural phenomena in mind. Job 5, 7 "Sparks wing their way upward." Add also Jeremiah 18, 14.

Proceeding to the next class, that of the vegetable world we meet proverbs found in the books of the Bible other than the distinctively gnomic books. The proverb of the sour grapes—Jer. 31, 29. the relation of the straw to the corn Jer. 23, 28. the two fables, the one of Judges 9, 8-15 of the vine and olive and the fig and the bramble and the other parable in 2 Kings, 14 of the thistle of Lebanon. Besides the examples given by Koenig there ought to be added the section in the praise of wisdom in Sira 24, 12-17. Job 8, 11, "Can the bulrush shoot up without the mire, can the meadow grass grow up without the water?"

From the animal kingdom material is drawn for the following: Jer 13, 23 "Can the Ethiopian change his skin or the leopard his spots?"; the saying in Ec. 9, 4 "Better is a live dog than a dead lion." The bee gives a proverb to Ben Sira 11, 3 Proverbs does not mention it but where the Hebrew has the ant the Greek readers had inserted for them in the Septuagint after 6, 8 one on the bee. The flea is mentioned in the popular saying 1 Sam 24, 15. The partridge is the source of another 1 Sam 26, 20. Amos 3, 4 has the lion and the young lion. Amos 3, 5 has the bird but without close definition. Amos 5, 18 has the lion, the bear and the snake Habakuk 1, 14 has "keremes lo moshel bo." Job 6, 5-6 has the wild ass and the ox. Isaiah 1, 3 "The ox knoweth his master and the ass his master's crib" Jeremiah 8, 7 has a list of birds—the stork, the turtle dove, and two others. The gregarious habits of animals Ben Sira strikes off in 13, 15-17 and in 27, 9 "Birds of a feather flock together. As already indicated, the last is preserved in a quotation in Bab Ḳam. 92b where it is actually quoted as being from the Ketubim (See Schechter J. Q. R. Vol 3 p690). Curious is the combination which the Yalḳuṭ gives מה לחבן כל עוף למינו ישכון ובן אדם לדומה לו (Sira) (Jer) את חבר where we have the combination of Jeremiah and Sira introduced by "hakatuv omer" a phrase limited to introduce Bible quotations (ib. 699). A similar Talmudic proverb reads לא לחנם הלך הזרזיר אצל הערב אלא מפני שהוא מינו "Not without reason does the starling go to the raven, they are of a class" or in the opposite form לא הלך עורב אצל זרזיר אלא שהוא מינו Ber. Rab. 65. See also Tanḥuma Vayera קרב לגבי אדיתנא ואיודחן and the Yalḳuṭ Toledoth near end מטייל ואזיל רוקלא בישתא גבי קינא דשרכי Further proverbs are furnished by the eagle, Ezekiel 17, 3-10 since the selection is called expressly in the text, a mashal, by the serpent, Sira 25, 15 by the scorpion 26, 7 dragon 25, 16 wolf 13, 18 dog Pro 26, 11 and 1 Sam 24, 15 ox Pro 14, 1.

The proverbs drawn from the life of man can best be handled as far as the social relationships are concerned when we deal with the general concepts as well as those drawn from the religious concepts. The proverbs coming from the arts and crafts can be entered here. Such are Proverbs 25, 11 "Apples of gold in figures of silver a word spoken in proper manner" and its parallel in Ben Sira 26, 18 "Golden pillars upon sockets of silver, fair feet with a constant heart." So also Ben Sira 2, 5 "For gold is tried in the fire" and Pro 27, 17 "Iron is hardened by iron" to which might be added Pro 27, 21 "The firing pot for silver and the furnace for gold, a man proved according to his praise and its counterpart in Sira 28, 5 "The furnace proves the potters vessel, the trial of a man is his discourse." Sira 32, 6 "a seal ring of carbuncle set in gold" also Proverbs 26, 24 "Like silver dross laid over an earthen vessel." These are, wherever given, by Koenig, entered in the mineral class. But the writer is not interested so much in the mineral part of it as he is in the art side. Therefore they are entered here in the fourth division.

5. Concepts

Beginning with the Concept of God, we find that Sira and Proverbs agree in the main points. In Chap 42, 15 Ben Sira gives the praise of the Creator. We have here emphasized the unity of God—"From everlasting is he one." He lives and endures forever 23,9. "Through His word of command all things were formed," reading in 42, 15c with the text and the marginal reading באומר אלהים מעשיו נוצרו compare with this Ps 33, 6 בדבר ה' שמים נעשו This form of the thought is quite frequent in Hebrew Literature. The Baruch Sheamar prayer in the liturgy—"Blessed is He who spoke and the world came into being. Blessed is He who made the creation" (בראשית has, in the phrasing of the later literature, become a technical term indicating creation. The word is then used even with the b prefixed. This of course arose from the position of bereshith as the first word in the Bible and as the first word of the creation account. A similar use is to be seen in another part of the liturgy. "In his goodness he reneweth every day the work of bereshith." How old this usage is can be seen from Sira 15, 14 Hebrew text "Elohim mibereshith bara adam.") The fifth chapter of the Pirke Aboth "By ten words was the world created"; and references in the oldest strata of Rabbinic literature, Sifiri, Vayhi Binsoa, amply prove this. In addition see also Tanḥuma, Vayaḳhel 8 (page 131 of the Warsaw ed) also Aboth de Rabbi Nathan 27, 1 and 38, 12 at end, also Seder Eliyahu Zuta where the phrasing of the Baruch Sheamar prayer is given, also Erubin 13b, Sanhedrin 19, Shemoth Rab 25, etc. To Him belongs the knowledge of the deepest and the highest (verse 18) of the past and of the future חליפות ונקיות Nothing can be added to Him, and nothing can be taken away from Him. His wisdom is His own and He needs no instructor. This idea is paralleled by Is. 40, 14. "With whom did He take counsel and who gave Him understanding." The fragments of the gnomic literature scattered through the canon give the same estimate. 1 Sam 14, 6—"For there is nothing to prevent the Lord from saving through many or through few." God sees all—"For not as man sees does the Lord see—for man sees according to the outward seeming, but God sees to the heart" 1 Sam 16, 7. Sira's description of nature, sun, moon, stars, rainbow, snow, lightning, cloud, thunder through which he seeks to show the great power of God, though beautiful, stands below Job in artistic merit. The phrase which at first sounds pantheistic 43, 27 וקץ דבר הוא הכל "And the end of the matter, He is the all," is hardly so. The very next phrase denies the identification. It means rather that all qualities are His and therefore sums up the attempt to give all the attributes since no other adequate praise of God is possible. There is another such passage in a later didactic poem—the Shir Hayyiḥud, the song of the Unity. In the canto for the third day of the week, there occur the following lines סובב הכל ומלא את הכל ובהיות הכל אתה בכל which might be rendered in the following pantheistic sense—"Thou surroundest the all and fillest the all and when the all exists thou art in the all." That to the later writers this possibility suggested itself is proven by the fact that the lines have been attacked for what was to them an evident pantheism. But the border line is far off. The pantheistic phraseology had not yet reached such perfection. By kol the writer does not mean the "All" at all. He has reference to some such Biblical phrase as the "Male *kol* haaretz kevodo"—the whole earth is full of his glory. Isaiah 6, 3.

The gnomic Psalms have involved in them a statement of revelation. These Psalms have placed God in the position of the ḥacham of the proverbs. So in Ps 50, 15-20 we have God himself instructing the wicked and reproving them. In the revelation of God to man, Sira and Proverbs differ markedly. Both of them talk of wisdom and both of them personify it. The praise of wisdom is to be found in longer or shorter extracts in every "Wisdom book." Proverbs can say of it that wisdom was with the Creator "when yet there were no depths," "before the mountains were yet sunk down," "when he prepared the heaven" and "happy is the man that findeth me" for "he findeth life and obtaineth favor from the Lord" (8 passim). Job 28, 20-28 also has a description of wisdom. But neither Job nor Proverbs take the step which Sira takes. Wisdom by him is regarded not in the sense of teaching or instruction or of empirical knowledge, for that Proverbs has also, but in the sense of the later Jewish development—the law of Moses, or even of the Torah in the later sense. With Sira, other books of the Apocrypha share this notion. Baruch has the equation "Wisdom is the Torah." To the other nations God did not give knowledge, only to Jacob did he show the way of wisdom. (3, 29—35) This is the position of Sira throughout. In chapter 24, in the description of wisdom, parallel to Proverbs 8 and 9, Wisdom is made to say "So the creator of all things gave me a commandment and He that made me caused my tabernacle to rest and said 'Let thy dwelling be in Jacob and thine inheritance in Israel.' He created me in the beginning" (the Hebrew text must have had here not merosh or me'olam, but the almost technical mibereshith, compare a similar use in Sira 15, 14 hence the possibility of saying mibereshith) "before the world" (for the thought compare Ber. Rab, 1.1 where Proverbs is interpreted in the same style.) "And I shall never fail. Likewise in the city of Jerusalem was my power and I took root in an honorable people, even in the portion of the Lord's inheritance" (compare Deut 31, 9).

But far more explicit is this—"All these things are the covenant of the Most High God, even the law which Moses commanded for an heritage unto the congregation of Jacob." In Proverbs, the name Moses does not occur.

After this statement of Sira, his doctrine of the immortality of Israel is clear. "The days of Israel cannot be numbered" 37, 25 (compare this Shir Hashirim Rab. "Yisrael en lahem beṭelah o'amim") Sira's identification of the Law with Wisdom shows itself clearly in the section devoted to the praise of the fathers. Here he reviews the course of Jewish history very briefly (for another passage in praise of the fathers see 1 Mac 2 51-63 but there the author has an entirely different aim. There the writer is interested in showing the reward of righteousness and obedience to the law of God, etc., as exemplified in the lives of the fathers) but dwells lovingly upon Aaron, 44, 6 describing his vestments, the offerings and his consecration. He even looks upon the rebellion of Dathan and Abiram as a rebellion against Aaron. With similar loving touch, he describes the High Priest Simon. His description is the type of those given in the middle ages by the poets of the liturgy, in the ritual of the Day of Atonement, when the description of the services at the temple on that day forms an important part of the services. The love of the ceremonial side of religion is already here to be seen. This is the beginning. His day was already productive of the beginnings of the later Talmudic ramifications. For such a beginning see his saying—"He that washeth himself after touching a dead body, if he touch it again what availeth his washing" 34, 25. But there are indications in Sira of that other side—the study of the law is becoming, what it did actually become later, study for the pure love of the law (39, 1-5).

The breach of the law, according to Sira (and man has the power to choose, 15, 11-17), the forsaking of wisdom, according to Proverbs (hence sinner=fool and sin=folly, kesil, iveleth and kesiluth are found only in gnomic literature, evil is found only four times outside of the gnomic books, otherwise it also is limited to them) constitutes a sin. Since this is ultimately connected with the thought that God is righteous and just, the result of sin is ever the same, and both Sira and the Proverbs as well as the gnomic Psalms have the same outlook. The righteous man insures happiness to himself and even to his children after him—Pro 20, 7 "He who walketh with integrity is a righteous man, happy his children after him." He is delivered from distress, Pro 11, 8—also Job 5, 19. "The righteousness of the upright will save them Pro. 11, 6. The fruit of righteousness is a tree of life 11, 30. Behold the righteous man is recompensed on earth 11, 31. The gift of the Lord remaineth with the godly and his favor bringeth prosperity forever" Sira 11, 7. Conversely, sin and wickedness lead to punishment and death; see Pro. 11 passim and the extensive description of the misfortune befalling the wicked in Job 15, 20-35 as well as Chapter 12. Even if for a time punishment be delayed, it must come. Ps 27, 12 Pro 24. 19-20. "Fret not thyself because of the evildoers, nor be thou envious of the wicked for there will be no future for the evil man." "The lamp of the wicked will be quenched." However, there is a recognition of the possibility of a return through repentance, followed by forgiveness by God, for he is merciful. Sira 28, 2; 2, 11; and Pro 1, 20-33. In this repentance, in the gnomic writers sacrifice takes little part. For this see Ecc. 4, 17 "And it is nearer (to the thing pleasing to God) to listen than to bring the sacrifice of fools,"*[121] 1 Sam 15, 22 "Behold to obey is better than sacrifice, to attend better than the fat of rams," Amos 5, 24; Micah 6, 7-8. Note also at the end of Job 28 which was throughout a gnomic section, the saying—"And he hath said to man 'Behold the fear of the Lord, that is wisdom and turning from evil, that is understanding'." Similarly we should not be misled by the misfortunes of the righteous, for in the first place, it can only be temporary Pro 24, 16 "For seven times the righteous man may fall but rise, but the wicked shall stumble because of their evil" and Psalms "Even if he should fall he will not be swept away, for the Lord will support his hand." The schemes of the wicked, devised against the righteous react on themselves. Ps 7, 15-18. In the second place we have introduced by Proverbs the very striking thought 3, 11-12 "Because whomsoever the Lord loveth he admonisheth and as a father he delighteth in his son." Compare with this Ps 34. 20 Job 5, 17. All such trials are intended to refine and to polish for "Gold is tried in the fire and acceptable men in the furnace of adversity" Sira 2, 5. That raison d'etre for adversity and suffering is quite common in later Jewish Literature and covers both individual and communal suffering. See Menaḥoth 5b "The olive yields its oil only under pressure, so Israel gains his good powers through suffering." See also Berachoth 5 "Three gifts God gave to Israel and all of them through suffering." For this suffering the Talmudic writers have the phrase "Yissurin shel ahabah." As for the direct connection between suffering and sin see Aboth Chap 5 paragraph 11.

One important point should be noted—Proverbs does not know of an immortality. Sayings that death was the end all were too common not to have had their effect. Ps 30, 10; 6, 6; 88, 11-13; 89, 49; all point in the one direction. But neither does Sira know of an immortality. In Chapter 41 Sira had a splendid opportunity of introducing the thought. He speaks there of the bitterness of death to the man living at ease, in prosperity and happiness. But he gives no hint as to his belief in this matter. The most that he will concede is the immortality of Israel, and that, as can be seen, is a different kind of immortality. See Sira 37, 25—חיי איש מספר ימים וחיי עם ישראל ימי אין מספר

Yet in the other wisdom book of the Apocrypha, the Wisdom of Solomon, the belief is given in unmistakable terms, for example, 2, 23 "For God hath created man to be immortal, and made him to be an image of his own eternity" 2 Mac 7, 14 and 14, 46 have statements of the immortality, more, in the latter passage there is even included the resurrection of the body. Sira seems to have antedated the burning question which was one of the dividing lines between Pharisee and Saducee, but by the time of the Second Mac, that is, towards the end of the first century B. C. the position was already an established one. At any rate the thought of the Wisdom of Solomon and of 2 Mac gives a turn to the old theological question צדיק. ורע לו "For though they may be punished in the sight of man, yet is their hope full of immortality 3, 4 a thought frequently paralleled in later Rabbinic Literature.

The religious tone of Ben Sira is invigorating. Compared with it, Proverbs is even secular. Never does Proverbs turn into a real prayer. We have the petition in Pro 30, 7-9, but Sira prays and knows how to pray. He is anxious moreover that the God whom he worships, should be recognized by all the nations around. "Let them know Thee as we have known Thee that there is no God but only Thou, O God." 36, 1-5. This is typical of the whole spirit of the day. The proselytizing tendency (see Schürer Ges des Jud. Volkes, Edition 3, Leipzig 1898, Vol 3, pp. 1-135) gave rise to this verse of Ben Sira. The attitude that he assumes man must take toward God is well pointed out in 34, 20 "Whoso bringeth an offering of the goods of the poor doeth as one that killeth the son before the father's eye"—a clear expression of the social righteousness which brings the prophets and the proverb writers to the same ideal. The liturgical forms of both Church and Synagogue, in their insistence on the fatherly relationship of God and the necessity of social bond and union are therefore not without more ancient models.

With this thought of the brotherhood of man, we can easily pass on to the duties that one man owes another. Both Proverbs and Sira teach kindness, especially to the defenseless, the widow, the orphaned and the poor. Indeed in Sira, Charity has already the term by which it is called in later Rabinnic literature—ṣedaḳah 3, 30 where it scarcely means simply righteousness as is seen by the following verse in Chapter 4. The term is already on the border line, so much so that the Rabbis interpret it here too to mean charity. (Pro, 14, 34—Bab Bathra 13b; Pro. 10, 2—Rosh Hash. 16b) but in that case it may be looked upon as a projection backwards into the writings of the past of the thought of the later writer. For only in later times did that element of the root notion of ṣadaḳ gain emphasis. "Do not distress the poor for the cry of the poor shall be heard" Sira 4, 6. Forgiveness is taught in the way of an imitatio dei. Sira 28, 2—"Forgive thy neighbor the hurt he hath done thee, so shall thy sins also be forgiven when thou prayest. One man beareth hatred against another, and doth he seek pardon from the Lord? He showeth no mercy to a man which is like himself, and doth he ask forgivness for his sins?" Qualities which make it impossible for men to live together in peace and harmony are condemned—backbiting Sira 28, 2; Pro 11, 3; and compare Leviticus 19, 16—pride Sira 10, 7 and 12; Pro 8, 13;—humility is commended Sira 3, 18; Pro 3, 34. In both books licentiousness and unchastity are dealt with in strong disapproving terms. Both books presuppose monogamy.

As for the position of women, Pro 31 places it very high, though there are some passages which do not deal kindly with the troublesome woman.*[117] Sira has the same view. In general the Rabbis have a more exalted opinion of womankind. With children Sira recommends harshness. The daughter gives the greatest anxiety—hence Sira 7, 24-25 (see 69a). The child must be handled with vigor or else he will bring trouble to the parents. Sira 29, 1. The care and honoring of parents are enjoined Sira 3.

The social conditions in the proverbial literature vary. The conditions drawn from the fragments in the literature point to very early conditions. The parables certainly belong to conditions attendant upon agricultural life, with war which is possible of course at any period. But as we proceed we find the arts and crafts opening out. Ps 118, 22 has a builders proverb—"The stone which the builders have rejected hath become the corner stone." Isaiah 45, 9-10 has the pottery industry in mind. "Shall the clay say to the potter what doest thou and thy work if he has no hands." Jeremiah 18, 6 "We are as the clay in the hands of the potter." Isaiah has the carpenter. The general condition of the hired man is referred to in Job 7, 1-2. Haggai 1, 6 "He who does gain anything will be as one gaining (or putting his wage) into a bag with holes." Agriculture of course gives its quota. Amos 6, 12 "Will horses run upon the rock, or will a man plow the sea with oxen." Job 31, 40 refers to the unreliability of crops. The same notion is turned by Isaiah 5, 2, 4 to good account in portraying the meagre returns from the Lord's vineyard. Job 8, 11 "Can the bulrush shoot upward without mire, can the meadow grass grow up without water" has the same agricultural source. In Isaiah 28, 23-29 again agricultural conditions. The riddle of Samson Judges 14, 18, "If ye had not plowed with my heifer, etc.," ought to be included. The vintage gives the proverb to Obadiah 5 as well as to Jeremiah 49, 9 Sira takes a derogatory view of trades and is therefore decidedly inferior to the thought of the Talmudic authorities who extolled manual labor and made it obligatory upon every man to teach his son an honest trade. The commercial life, that through Greek spirit was coming into Palestine he condemns, 31, 15. But in this respect he agrees with the spirit of the pentateuchal legislation and with the attitude of the Rabbis. ולא כל המרבה בסחורה מחכים (Aboth and see also Sira 38, 24.) See Genizah Fragments J. I. R. Vol. 16, page 13, line 18—מרבה הונו ומחסר חכמתו איך ינקה מפני וו'

As for the political conditions the two canonical books are about the same. In both books we read of a king who is theoretically always wise. Sira 10. Him the Lord has chosen to rule over his people and when he is righteous the land will prosper. As the king, so the people Pro 29, 12. But there are indications that the theoretically perfect king was in actuality rather faulty and there are little remarks here and there which go to show that administration was not always running smoothly. "An unwise king destroyeth his people" Sira 10, 3. Sometimes through the poverty of the land, the representatives of the majesty and the might of the king went hungry. Sira 26, 28. Of the learned classes, Sira knows the scribe and the physician. Despite the fact that he says "He who runneth before his maker let him fall into the hand of the physician" 38, 15,*[118] he can still say "Honor the physician with the priest and give him his portion as it is commanded thee."*[119] The hostility to the physician is expressed in another one of the gnomic books—in the Aboth di Rabbi Nathan.*[120] The man who meets with most favor in his eyes is the man who gives his mind to the study of the Law of the Most High, 39, 1. His duty it is—lehagdil Torah ulhaadirah—"to increase the Law and to glorify it."

Notes

1. It is possible that here the author is quoting an old proverb and providing it with a running commentary.

2. "Skin for skin" and perhaps also the rest of the verse (although that might be regarded as an explanation of the short saying which had lost its original force and therefore the author felt the explanation necessary) must have been used originally in a sense parallel to Exodus 21, 24-25 "Eye for eye, tooth for tooth."

3. See Delitzsch, Assyrisches Handwörterbuch, Leipzig, 1896 p 431.

4. Id. p. 432.

5. Jeremiah 31, 28. אבות אכלו בסר ושני בנים תקהינה Ezekiel 18, 2 אבות יאכלו בסר ושני הבנים תקהינה The LXX Ed. Swete, Cambridge 1899) does not make any distinctions and renders both alike, with the exception of the rendering for תקהינה where the Hebrew is the same in Jeremiah and Ezekiel. Jr. 31, 29. *Ὁι πατέρες ἔφαγον ὄμφακα καὶ οἱ ὀδόντες τῶν τέκνων ἡμωδίασαν* Ezekiel has instead of *ἡμω*—*ἐγομφίασαν*.

6. ר׳ אבין קרא עליה אבות יאכלו בסר ושני בנים תקהינה והן קוראין על אבותיהם אבותינו חטאו ואינם ואנחנו עונותיהם סבלנו.

7. 1 Sam 19, 24 has the mere statement of the proverb as arising out of Saul's presence among the "sons of the prophets." 1 Sam 10, 12 on the other hand is an attempted explanation as to the reason and origin of the proverb. The starting point for the understanding of the proverb is to be found in the acknowledged surprise at finding Saul in his present company. One or the other, Saul or his prophetic associates, is of a distinctly inferior rank and the difference is recognized by the people. But which one,

Saul or the prophets, is the inferior? The LXX by its rendering καὶ τίς πατὴρ αὐτοῦ for the Massoretic text ומי אביהם leans to the side of the prophets. Saul is not so much superior, if at all, "for who is his father." So the Syr. and Vulg, render.

Smith, International Critical Commentary, Samuel, New York, 1899, pp 70-71 does not give a definite decision on this point. He thinks that the LXX reading gives little help, but leans to the opinion that the surprise is expressed because Saul, the son of a well to do man should be found in the company of the wandering prophets.

Budde, Kurzer Hand Kommentar zum Alten Testament Tübingen. 1902. in loco, does not accept the LXX, Syr and Vulgate rendering. "Wahrscheinlicher ist die umgekehrte auffassung-Saul als Kind guter Eltern sollte sich doch mit solch hergelaufenen Leuten abgeben."

Klosterman, Kurzgefaster Kommentar. Nördlingen, 1897, in loco. is too far fetched in his attempt to see the popular etymology for נביא as being אין אבי.

Driver, Notes to the Hebrew Text of the Books of Samuel, Oxford 1890, follows the Hebrew—"who is their father" i. e. is their father more likely than Kish to have had a son a prophet. Prophetic inspiration is no hereditary inspiration.

The commentators do not allow for the fact that there might have been, as there probably was, an earlier and a later interpretation. The earlier would have spoken against the prophets, who at that time were at their very beginnings and had no actual accomplishments recorded to their credit. The later account would have felt that Saul was hardly worthy of the companionship of the prophets.

8. Jeremiah 8, 7.

9. The Old Testament in Greek According to the Septuagint, Swete, Cambridge 1899.

10. Duhm, Das Buch Jesaia, Handkommentar zum Alten Testament, Göttingen 1902.

11. Marti, Kurzer Hand Kommentar Tübingen, 1900, in loco.

12. Cheyne, The Prophecies of Isaiah. London 1884, in loco.

13. Dillman, Der Prophet Isaiah, Leipzig, 1890, in loco.

14. Orelli, Kurzgefaster Kommentar, Munich 1891.

15. Hitzig, Die Prophetischen Bücher des Alten Testament, Leipzig, 1854.

16. Die Sprüche, Hand Kommentar zum Alten Testament, Göttingen 1898.

17. Die Sprüche erklärt. Kurzer Handkommentar. Freiburg, 1897.

18. Toy, Proverbs, International Critical Commentary, New York, 1899.

19. עד מתי פתים תאהבו פתי ולצים לצון חמדו להם וכסילים ישנאו דעת.

20. Cheyne, Prophecies of Isaiah, London 1884.

21. Duhm. Das Buch Jesaia, K. H. zum Alten Testament, Göttingen 1902.

22. The תושיה passages are the following:

Proverbs 2, 7; 18, 1; 3, 21; 8, 14.

Job 5, 12; 6, 13; 11, 6; 12, 16; 26, 3; 30, 22.

23. The עצה passages are more numerous. It occurs 87 times in all, 29 of this number being found in Proverbs, Job and Psalms.

24. The parallelism can be seen by comparison of the columns

Isaiah 33.		Psalms 15.	
מי יגור לנו אש אוכלה, מי יגור לנו מוקדי עולם	14.	1.	מי יגור באהליך מי ישכון בהר קדשך
הלך צדקות ודבר מישרים,	15a.	2.	הלך תמים ופעל צדק ודובר אמת בלבבו כספו לא נתן בנשך ושחד על נקי לא לקח
מאס בבצע מעשקות נער כפיו מתמך בשחד אטם אזנו משמע דמים ועצם עיניו מראות ברע	15b.		לא רגל על לשונו לא עשה לרעהו רעת וחרפה לא נשא על קרובו מי ישכן בהר קדשך:
הוא מרומים ישכן	16.		

Duhm, above quoted, denies the parallelism and takes 15b as an interpolation, but the parallelism exists outside of 15b.

25. The LXX has for צדיק ἀδικως but that manifestly cannot be the rendering for צדיק.

Cheyne, "Can the prey be taken from the mighty one, or the captive of the terrible one escape." The prophecies of Isaiah, London 1884. Hitzig keeps the reading צדיק. Orelli has "statt צדיק lies nach Syr. Vulg. mit vielen anderen עריץ."

Dillman-Most of the commentators have interpreted the גבור to be the Chaldean; in that case צדיק cannot be interpreted, for while it may mean "victor," it always implies, besides, the notion of "right," therefore they must necessarily change צדיק to עריץ. Dillman (as does Marti, K Hk zum A. T.) takes גבור to refer to God and then צדיק could stand as the Massoretic text has it. But against Dillman it can be urged that if גבור and צדיק mean God, the next verse cannot be interpreted. From God it would be supposed that nothing could possibly escape. But the answer to the question "can the prey be taken from the mighty one" is that the prey will actually escape. גבור and צדיק must therefore refer, at least, to some human being, from whom escape may be possible but hardly likely. The qualities of this human are emphasized to be such that one would hardly expect that what he was seized should ever be able to escape his clutches and actually regain freedom. The כי and the גם are in place in the text and are of importance, besides. You would not expect that such and such would happen but, כי, it does happen.

Duhm, Das Buch Jesaia Hk. zum Alten Testament Göttingen 1902, adopts the reading עריץ.

26. Duhm, Das Buch Jeremia, Kurzer hand kommentar Tübingen 1901, in loco. "9, 22-23 ist ein harmlos unbedeutender spruch."

Hitzig, Der Prophet Jeremia, 2nd Ed. Leipzig 1866 calls attention to the recurrences of the three ideals חסד

צדקה ומשפט in Ps. 33, 5. But that all points to the gnomic origin of the section in Jeremiah. That does not mean necessarily that the Prophet borrowed the passage bodily, or even that he had some text before him which he altered slightly in order to make it fit the purposes for which he intended it. It only implies the presence of a literature, with distinctive vocabulary and terminology. Part of that literature to be sure was only in the making. It was still in the speech of the folk. But part of it must most assuredly have been written. Giesebricht, Das Buch Jeremia, Gottingen 1894, in loco—"eine Gnome." Because of its gnomic character it of course necessarily falls out of alignment with the rest of the chapter in Jeremiah. But that does not argue against its authenticity as a part of Jeremiah's writing. It fits in with the opinions of Jeremiah as well as anywhere else. Comparison with Isaiah 60, 18 and the use of the root there (תהלה) shows that הלל was used of the "war cry," the "cry of victory." Marti Kurzer Hk in loco has "Ruhm," "weil sie den Heiden Einlass gewähren, die mit ihren Gaben den Ruhm der Stadt bezeugen" but this does not carry out the figure of war in the verse implied. Of course there is no doubt that תהלה later means praise and that therefore "Renown," Cheyne, Prophecies of Isaiah, in loco, is correct as far as it goes. But 1 Kings 20, 11 also points the way to the military use of the word יתהלל. This interpretation is strengthened by the use of ישועה in Isaiah 60, 18. That is undoubtedly a military phrase, see Isaiah 26, 1; 52, 7; 59, 17. Ps. 118, 15 where ישועה is used with קול רנה Ex. 15, 2; 14, 13; 2Ch. 20, 17 etc.

27. Genizah Fragments Jewish Quarterly Review Vol. 16; of the Ms. p. 5 line 14ff.

אל יתהלל אדם ביפיו ותארו
אל יתהלל בהמון משפחתו
אל יתהלל אדם בכח גבורתו
אל יתהלל אדם בכבוד עשרו

אל יתהלל אדם ברב חכמתו
כי אם לבטוח ולהתהלל בי״י
לעשות צדקה וחסד
כי בצדקה אדם ינצל

ועל ישע על בינתו
בהשכל (וידוע) יוצרו
ולסגות תמיד באמרי שפר
ואין מידו מציל

ולא ישמח ללא דבר
כי במה נחשבים חם
כי אם לכבוש את יצרו
כי אינם יכולים להצילו

28. Ps 1, 3.

והיה כעץ שתול על פלגי מים אשר
פריו יתן בעתו ועלהו לא יבול
וכל אשר יעשה יצליח

Jeremiah 17, 8.

והיה כעץ שתול על מים ועל יובל
ישלח שרשיו ולא ירא כי יבא חם
והיה עלהו רענן ובשנת בצרת לא
ידאג ולא ימיש מעשות פרי

29. Carmel, by its location, striking and impressive, would easily lend itself to figurative usages. The precipitous break at the sea accented its height. Tabor also was marked out by its location on the northern face of the plain of Esdraelon, for the poet's figures. See Smith, Historical Geography of Palestine, New York, 1903, Tenth Ed. pp 340. "Carmel is visible not only from the hills of Samaria, from Jaffa, from Tyre, from Hermon, from the hills of Naphtali but also from the hills behind Gadara, East of the Jordan and from many other points in Gilead." For Tabor see page 417.

30. The LXX (Swete B) reads *οἱ λεγόντες Οὐχὶ προσφάτως οἰκαδόμηνται αἱ οἰκιάι; αὕτη ἐστιν ὁ λέβης ἡμεῖς δὲ τὰ κρέα* Kretzschmar, Handkommentar zum Alten Testament, Göttingen, 1900, renders the passage as follows "Die da sprechen 'Sollten wir uns nicht den Töchtern der Stadt Jerusalem (geschlechtlich) nahen?' Ist sie doch der Topf und wir das Fleisch?" His commentary starts with b. The pot is the city, those who live in it are secure and safe from the flames. There is also a certain implied superiority over those who were carried away into exile. He therefore suggests that the full statement of the second half was, by comparison with Ezekiel 24, 10 העיר הסיר המרק ואנחנו הבשר K. suggests קרב in the sexual sense and takes בתים as an abbreviation for בת ירושלים.

Smend, Der Prophet Ezechiel, Leipzig, 1880, also makes b the starting point of the commentary "die jedenfalls die

1 versh. motivirt" and, as Kretzschmar, makes it imply security on the part of those who are in the city.

Ewald reads with the Septuagint, but he does not consider necessary the change of לא into הלא. Smend, because the rendering of Ewald does not agree with Ezekiel 24, renders, "It is not yet at the building stage we have much to suffer from the fires of war."

Hitzig, Der Prophet Ezechiel, Leipzig 1847, says that the לא cannot equal הלא. The leaders are thinking of making war, and therefore insist that the proper time for building is not the present.

Orelli, Das Buch Ezechiel Munich 1896, takes it as a statement of the war party. We have the war to think about first.

Bertholet, Das Buch Hezekiel, Freiburg, 1897, agrees with Cornill who follows the LXX, reading הלא מקרוב נבנו הבתים.

The houses have been rebuilt are we not safe?

Of the Jewish commentators Rashi, takes b as implying security.

היא הסיר ואנחנו הבשר כשם שאין הבשר יוצא מן הסיר עד גמר בשולו כך לא נצא ממנה עד שנמות.

The first part he understands as being elliptical האומרים לא בקרוב יבואו דברי הנביאים: בנות בתים אין לחוש להם אלא בנות בתים ושבת בתוכם כי לא נגלה מן העיר הזאת עד מותנו.

Kimḥi agrees with Rashi in assuming the first part elliptical. The rendering of Kretzschmar of קרב in the sexual sense is too far fetched to be of any value here. Nor is it necessary to clog the interpretation by assuming that once a prophet uses a certain figure he has to develop it in exactly the same fashion in every other chapter of the book. It is mechanical to say that the phrase here must coincide with the other pot passage in Ezekiel 24. The key to the interpretation lies in verse 7. The prophet's answer would be without point if we could not assume that the men of

Jerusalem have been saying all along that they could not be removed from the city. Jerusalem is now to remain and those who live in it are safe. Ezekiel's answer is the only permanent ones are those whom you have slain in the city. The living shall be carried forth. Hence 3b must be taken to indicate fancied security on the part of those who would begin designs for the rebuilding and refortifying of Jerusalem 3a we read in accordance with the LXX with הלא.

31. Ewald Propheten, 2nd Edition, Vol 2. Göttingen 1868.

32. Cornill, Der Prophet Ezekiel, 1886.

33. Bernholet, Das Buch Hezekiel, Freiburg, 1889.

34. Kretzschmar, Handkommentar zum Alten Testament, Göttingen 1900.

35. Harper, Amos and Hosea, International Critical Commentary, New York, 1905. "The prophet introduces the new strophe with one of the many wise sayings which were familiar to him, moral sayings which constituted the stock in trade of the wise men who sat at the gate. Other examples of the use of the wisdom sayings may be found in 4, 1b, 14d; 6, 4b; 8, 7a; 10, 12f; 14, 9."

36. Harper, above quoted.

37. Nowack Die Kleine Propheten, Handkommentar zum Alten Testament. The LXX Ed. Swete, B. rearranges the last phrase of the verse. It reads *και ο λαος ο συνιων συνεπλεκετο μετα πορνης*. What it did seems to be to have taken the אם זנה of the next verse, read it עם זנה and added it to 14d.

Nowack takes it as a fragment, occurring elsewhere and inserted here, but he does not indicate the only possible source for such a statement-proverbial literature.

Harper, Amos and Hosea, International Critical Commentary, renders "Yea, a people stupid and falling to ruin" but the לא יבין is relative and ילבט is the main verb.

Gardner's emendation (A. J. S. L. Vol 18, p 79) ועם מנאפים ילבטו is mere conjecture.

This much must be granted. ועם לא יבין ילבט does not go with the preceding assertions made in the verse. It is evidently an addition. It might possibly be the second half of 4, 11 and the complete proverb would then read זנות ויין ותירוש יקח לב ועם לא יבין ילבט.

39. Swete Ed. B.

40. Marti, Kurzer Hk 1903.

41. Michaelis, Deutsche Ubersetzung des Alten Testament, 1872.

Emendation accepted by Nowack, Harper and Marti.

42. König Stylistik, Poetik und Rhetorik, Leipzig, 1900.

Budde Z. A. T. W. 1882, 6ff.

See also Hebrew text of Ben Sira 38, 16b.

43. Briggs, Psalms, International Critical Commentary, New York, 1906.

44. Ehrlich.

45. ἐπιστηρῶ ἐπὶ σὲ τοὺς ὀφθαλμούς μου "Dasselbe Wort haben sie für עצה Proverbs 16, 30." (Baethgen Psalms, Hk zum Alten Testament). They therefore read אין עצה.

46. Baethgen, Psalms, Hk. zum A. T. in loco.

47. Duhm, Kurzer Hk. zum A. T. in loco.

48. מכריז: רבי אלכסנדרי מאן בעי חיי מאן בעי חיי כנוף ואתו כולי עלמא לגביה. אמרי ליה הב לן חיי אמר להו מי האיש החפץ חיים וגו'

See also Yalḳuṭ Shimoni, Paragraph 720 at end. See also Vayikra Rab. 16, 2.

49. Baethgen quotes Krochmal. The emendation of מהמון into מהון as suggested by Krochmal is confirmed by comparison with Tobit 12, 8b. See page 22 of the text.

50. See note 43.

51. Baethgen Psalms, in loco.

52. The LXX agrees with the Massoretic text except in that it evidently read שלהבתיה φλογες αυτης. Furthermore it has τον πανταβιον for את כל הון ביתו. Did it have the reading before it of את כל נפשו? The text as the Hebrew now has it

seems to be confirmed by Pro. 6, 30-31 where we have the same יבוזו and את כל הון ביתו.

שלהבתיה Budde (Kurzer Hk. Freiburg, 1898, in loco) quotes Bickell as suggesting שלהבות יקוד שלהבתיה; Ewald, Hitzig, Olshausen Kamphausen suggest the simple reduplication שלהבתיה שלהביה. This naturally would account for the present condition of the text. The scribe left out one of the words that, to his eye, were absolutely alike. The יה ending of the second is by these commentators taken to be the divine element. They render "Brandes Flammen sind ihre Flammen"—that is, the lightning, just as קול יהוה is the thunder.

Ibn Ezra has this comment—מחלקת בין אנשי המסורה אם היא מלה אחת או שתים והקרוב שהיא שתים וסמיכת השם כמו הררי אל:

He takes the word as being two words and the יה he also takes as the divine element. Another Hebrew commentator, Meẓudath Zion, also takes the יה as the divine element and adds that it is here used as it is in מאפליה Jer. 2, 31 to denote intensity. Other words with similar ending מרחביה מאפליה (see Gesenius Dict. s. v.) are treated in the same way. But it is hard to maintain any such interpretation in the face of a name like בקבוקיה where we have exactly the same formation. It is much preferable to take יה away from any relationship with the יה of God's name and simply look upon it as an emphatic ending. See Jastrow, Journal of Biblical Literature, 1894 pp 19ff. 101-127. The crux of the question is in the occurrence of the ending jah in Assyrian names. Delitzsch looks upon it as a personal prefix and not as a divine element. (The Lutheran Church Review 14, 196-201.) See also Clay the Amurru, the Home of the Northern Semites, Philadelphia, 1909, pp 202 ff.

53. See Steuernagel in Hk zum A. T. Joshua page 175.

54. Trumbull, The Threshhold Covenant, pp. 22, 51, 55.

Strack, Der Blutaberglaube, p 68.

55. 1 Sam, 26, 20. כי יצא מלך ישראל לבקש את פרעוש אחד
כאשר ירדף הקורא בהרים:
1 Sam 24, 15. אחרי מי יצא מלך ישראל אחרי מי אתה רודף
אחרי כלב מת אחרי פרעש אחד:

The LXX inserts in 1 Sam 26, 20 נפשי after לבקש. It reads ὅτι ἐξελήλυθεν ὁ βασιλεὺς Ισραὴλ ζητεῖν ψυχήν μου and it leaves out the את פרעוש אחד. In support of the LXX is the argument against the double comparison involved in the Massoretic text—the king pursues after David as a flee, as one hunts the partridge on the mountains. With נפשי moreover the את would be in place. The LXX to 1 Sam 24, 15 has both the dog and the flea proverb.

The פרעוש אחד of 1 Sam 26, 20 is an insertion in the nature of a reminiscence of the scribe or reader of 1 Sam 24, 15. Klosterman's insertion of כנשר in the text makes the figure complete, but the figure can stand without it. See Budde, Die Bücher Samuel, Kurzer Hk. Tübingen 1902. Driver, Notes to the Hebrew Text of the Books of Samuel, Klosterman, Die Bucher Samuelis and der Könige. Kurzgefaster Kommentar, Nördlingen, 1887. Smith, Samuel, International Critical Commentary, New York 1899.

56. LXX Swete B. ὅτι οὐχ ὡς ἐμβλέψεται ἄνθρωπος, ὄψεται ὁ θεός.

57. הכל חייבין בראייה חוץ מחרש שטה וקטן וטומטום ואנדריגינוס ונשים ועבדים שאינם משוחררים החיגר והסומא והחולה והזקן ומי שאינו יכול לעלות ברגליו:

58. אל יתהלל חגר כמפתח while it is possible with Kittel, Hk zum A. T. in loco. to limit the חגר to the putting on of the sword (see the full expression in 1 Sam. 17, 39; 25, 13 and Ps. 45, 4) it is preferable to regard it in the more general sense. Girding up the loins was the preparatory stage to labor, battle or to the march. The loosening of the girdle, or the opening of it, would be the sign that the battle, march or task of any kind was over and accomplished.

יתהלל cannot be disassociated from the Aramaic הילולא or the Assyrian alalu, to shout for joy. Here it means "to sing the chant of victory." In other words, "Let not the man who is just girding up his loins, to enter the battle, set up the song of victory as can one who has already loosened his girdle." In the sense of singing the הלל to oneself it comes to mean simply to boast. See Jeremiah 9, 22-23. Proverbs 20, 14; 25, 14. Psalms 52, 3. Pro. 27, 1 Jeremiah 49, 4. Ps 97, 7.

59. Talmud Babli. Sanhedrin 38b.
דא'ר רבי יוחנן כי הוה דריש ר' מאיר בפירקיה הוה דריש תילתא שמעתא תילתא אגדתא תילתא מתלי ואמר ר' יוחנן ג' מאות משלות שועלים היו לו לרבי מאיר ואנו אין לנו אלא שלוש :

60. Talmud Babli Succah 28a and Baba Bathra 134a. In both passages the reference is particularly directed towards the משלות שועלים as it was in the case of Rabbi Meir.

61. See Yalḳuṭ Shimoni to 2 Chron. 9, 1. paragraph 1085.

62. See Zunz, Zur Geschichte und Literatur 122ff. See also the letter of Maimonides to his son (אגרות ושאלות ותשובות Warsaw 1877 p 2 ff.) and also the opening chapter of the Pirḳe Derabbenu Haḳḳadosh.

63. Kautzsch edition. Die Apokryphen und Pseudepigraphen des Alten Testament, Tubingen 1900. For literature see Schürer Geschichte des Jüdischen Volkes in ZA Jesu Christu 3rd Edition Leipzig 1898. 3rd Vol. p 344.

64. Die Apokryphen und Pseudepigraphen des A. T. 1900.

65. Ibid.

66. Charles Taylor. Sayings of the Jewish Fathers. 2nd Edition Cambridge 1899.

67. S. Schechter, Aboth de Rabbi Nathan. Vienna 1887.

68. Nos 3-12 in the Sefer Halliḳuṭim edited by Dr. L. Grünhut, Jerusalem 1903. There are more in the שלשה ספרים נפתחים edited by Schönblum and in the 3rd Vol of the Beth Talmud, Vienna 1883.

69. Leopold Dukes, Rabbinische Blumenlese, Leipzig 1844.

70. ספר מלין דרבנן Lublin 1898.

71. ספר מבחר הפנינים Das Buch Mibhar Hapeninim des Rabbi Jedaja ben Abraham Bederaschi Penini, Text by Dessau and German translation by Hirsch Löwinsohn. Berlin 1842.

72. See Genizah Fragments. S. Schechter, Jewish Quarterly Review, Vol. 16 pp 425-442. In a later note (see page 776 of the same volume) Schechter makes corrections of בחמקה into בחכמה on page 443 and סמו into כמו on line 10 of page 434. Both of these were typographical errors. The Ms. has the correct reading in both cases. Through the courtesy and kindness of Dr. Schechter I was allowed to examine the manuscript and have noted the following corrections to the printed text. Of these corrections some are typographical errors, some are misreadings of the Ms and others deal with conjectures which on further examination of the Ms cannot be allowed or do not seem probable.

The Ms has 14 pages and I therefore refer to the Ms numbering 1 to 14.

Page 1. Line 2. It is rather clear that the text of a is כנזר מתאוה. וחמה nor is the דף of ויגדף invisible.

3b. תאות is clear. The last word is perhaps אכילה. The upper stroke of the ל is still to be seen and the vowel above (the Ms. is provided with the superlinear accents) is ˅. The context suggests the reading אכילה.

4b. So much is readable ושלות עולם מ(מה'.....חכמ)ים

5b. All that is visible is the first word וחמודתו.

6b. The first three letters are most probably לחש and not לחש.

7b. The reading is ורב א.....ות. The א belongs to the second word.

10b. b starts in from the margin. There is a space where a word might have been written. The top layer of the paper is gone. It is, therefore, to be inferred that the scribe had made a mistake, erased the word and then found that he could not write on the rough surface that the erasure had caused. He, therefore, began a little way in from the margin.

12a. Schechter reads שנואי but the Ms. has no ו and the vowels call for שנאי.

12b. The reading יכין is not possible. The last letter was evidently an ם and the vowel of the syllable was ˇ. Read יחכם.

15a. Very faint. Read אהב חכמה אהב וו'

16b. Read (וכבוד אנשים) בצע (ותאוה)

17b. וכבוד is clear at the beginning of the line.

18b. Read וכבוד קרובים אכילה ושתיה

18a. There is no ו before חכמה.

Page 2. 3a. The first word was probably אהבת

5b. Read ולא יתעדנו בטוב הגדול

16a. The text is as follows חכמים תממים קרובי אלהים Schechter suggests reading חסדים but the first letter is decidedly a ת.

17a. Read אהבה תלויה בבצע ואכילה

Page 4. Line 1a. The last word is most likely נבונים and not נכונים.

18— First word is תורה not תודה.

Page 6. Line 1b. The middle word is blotted and rubbed but it was most probably וידוע. See the passage in Jeremiah 8, 22-23 of which this is an elaboration.

3a. Schechter has the wrong division of words. Read כי בצדקה אדם ינצל instead of כי בצדק האדם ינצל

8b. The last word is דעה not רעה.

12a. במים not ממים.

Page 7. Line 2a. Schechter reads כי חמשה שערים נמצאים בכל החיים but the text ought to be כי חמשה שערים נמצאים בבעלי החיים.

Page 8. Line 2b. The Ms reads וחכמה בד נמצאים. On line three the scribe made a mistake and marked it by putting dots over the letters. דורש. The margin has the word דרישה. It is possible therefore that 2b read וחכמה בדרישת נמצאים.

10b. The last word is עמלו.

Page 9. Line 3a. Read תחלת יראה דעת יי׳.

Page 10. Line 1b. Ms reads פיו not פיהו.

Page 11. Line 5b. Ms reads מכשילים but this is a mistake for משכילים. See 6a.

12a. Read חנפש.

19a. מרבה קרח and not מרב הקרח.

Page 12. Line 6b. The last part is abraded. The Ms has ומלעבים על מש Schechter's conjecture of משפט is satisfactory but the vowel of the last word still visible was ˇ hence צדק is unsatisfactory. Read חכם.

11b. See Ezekiel 23, 35. The line ought to end with יי Read אחרי גוו ישלך יי׳.

Page 13. Line 18a. Read מרבה הונו ומחסר חכמתו

Page 14. Line 1. This line was constructed as was 18 on page 13. מרבה הונו opened the line. אם יעשה can be read in b. The line ended most probably with יש לו.

2a. The fragment of the מ and the חון show continuation of the construction.

2b. אולי תקוה perhaps with the same ending of יש לו.

3b. לא יבקה.

4b. Probably צדקתו עו(מדת לעד).

5b. Perhaps ועשרים בשפ(לות יפולו

6b. The Ms. has וגברי hence the ם can be safely conjectured.

9a. צריך אדם לדעת נפשו The עת are to be seen in the Ms. The point of the ל still is visible and the phrase is found in line 12.

9b. ולה to be seen in the Ms. The vowels however are clear and would point to a reading ולהתבונן.

11a. The Ms. reads הלב not חיב.

11b. The Ms. has ממטמו. The word can be easily supplied ממטמונים.

17b. The last word is וחכמה.

16b. The last word, or what is left of it, is צ. We want a word therefore ending in ו and in which the צ would have a short o. The word was most probably צרכו.

73. Cowley and Neubauer, the original Hebrew of a Portion of Ecclesisaticus. Introduction p 28, 29.

Dukes Blumenlese (above quoted) pages 31, 32, 67-84.

See literature in Jewish Encyclopedia Vol 2 p. 681 at end of article Ben Sira—Alphabets of.

74. LXX Swete B reads — ὅτι χαίρει πᾶσιν οἷς μισεῖ ὁ θεὸς συντρίβεται δε δι' ἀκαθαρσίαν ψυχῆς.

75. Editions of and Commentaries to Ben Sira. Cowley and Neubauer.

The Original Hebrew of a Portion of Ecclesiasticus, Oxford 1897.

Schechter and Taylor, The Wisdom of Ben Sira, Cambridge 1899.

Hebraische Text des Buches Ecclesiasticus.

Peters, Freiburg, 1902. Die Weisheit Jesus Sirach, Smend, Berlin 1906.

See Literature in Smend above quoted pp XII-XIII.

76. ארבעה אין הדעת סובלתן אלו הן דל גאה ועשיר מכחש וזקן מנאף ופרנס מתגאה על הציבור בחנם ויש אומרים אף המגרש את אשתו פעם ראשונה ושנית ומחזירה:

Immediately following this one there is another with a double ויש אומרים.

שלשה שונאין זה את זה אלו הן הכלבים והתרנוגלין והחברין ויש אומרים אף הזונות ויש אומרים אף תלמידי חכמים שבבבל:

77. Wildeboer, Kurzer Kommentar zum A. T. Proverbs, Introduction p XIII.

78. Frankenberg H. K. zum A. T. in loco.

79. Toy, Proverbs, International Critical Commentary. Introduction page XXX and with special reference to Pro. 30, 11.

80. Die Kleine Propheten, Nowack, HK zum A. T.

81. König, Stylistik, Poetik und Rhetorik. Leipzig 1900. page 163.

82. Harper Amos and Hosea in the International Critical Commentary.

83. Hastings, Dictionary of the Bible. Vol. 4 page 109.

84. Harper, Amos and Hosea, above quoted.

85. Wildeboer, Proverbs, above quoted, Introduction page XII.

86. See article, Languages of the Old Testament, Hastings, Dictionary of the Bible, Vol. 3. page 34 a, b and literature there cited.

87. See page 6 of text.

88. See reference on page 27 of text.

89. See note 72.

90. See Cheyne Job and Solomon page 118 ff, New York 1887. Toy, Proverbs, Introduction page XX.

91. Toy, Proverbs in loco.

92. Nowack, Die Kleine Propheten, Hk zum A. T. in loco.

93. LXX Ed. Swete B. ἐγκωμιαζομένων δικαίων ευφρανθήσονται λαοί ἀρχόντων δὲ ἀσεβῶν στένουσιν ἄνδρες.

94. Toy, Proverbs, in loco.

95. Jewish Quarterly Review, Genizah Fragments, Vol. 16, page 433 line 6.

96. Talmud Babli Baba Bathra 12a אמר אמימר וחכם עדיף מנביא

97. Cheyne, Job and Solomon, above quoted.

98. Hosea 4, 14d.

99. See Mishnah Yadayim Chapter 3. Mishnah 5.

100. See later Note 116.

101. Frankenberg Proverbs Hk zum Alten Testament, in loco.

102. Toy Proverbs, International Critical Commentary in loco.

103. Wildeboer, Proverbs Kurzer Hand K.

104. Toy Proverbs page 192.

105. Revised Version "that make a man an offender in a cause" or marginal reading "make men to offend by

their words." Marti, Jesaia Kurzer Hk, in loco, "sie sind מחטיאי אדם die Leute schuldig hinstellend בדבר, also die Denuncianten; man kann sich nur fragen, ob בדבר heissen soll'mit Worten, mit geschickter Verleumdung, oder nicht: um eines Wortes Willen." But opposed to this is that החטיא is not used in this sense of denounce or condemn. For the proper use of the Hiphil see 1 Kings 14, 16; 16, 13; 15, 30; 15, 26, 34; 16, 26; 22, 53. 2 Kings 3, 3; 10, 29, 31; 13, 2, 11; 14, 24; 15, 9, 18, 24, 28; 23, 15; 21, 16; 13, 6; 17, 21; Nehemiah 13, 26; Jer 32, 35; Eccl. 5, 5; Deut. 24, 4; 1 Kings 16, 2; 21, 22; 2 Kings 21, 11; Exodus 23, 36.

Duhm Isaiah Hand K. renders בדבר "with words" and interprets the whole phrase to mean "Menschen schuldig zu machen, als schuldig hinzustellen." Duhm therefore takes מחטיאי—מרשיעי but for this as noted above there is no parallel.

Dillman, Der Prophet Jesaia, Leipzig, 1890 sets aside the interpretation "die Leute schuldig sprechen in einer Rechtasche" also the interpretation "verurtheilen um eines Wortes Willen" and "die Leute verleiten mit Worten zu sündigen." He also maintains that החטיא cannot equal הרשיע.

Cheyne Prophecies of Isaiah, in loco is open to the same objection of misinterpretation of מחטיאי.

The reference is here undoubtedly to the משלי העם again, who have misled the people by their word—word being used in the technical sense, every phrase being called a דבר, for the proverbs are often called דברי חכמים, משלי חכמים being a much later phrase, see Ben Sira Hebrew text 3, 29—Neither has the second phrase any relationship with judicial matters. They lay snares for the reprover at the gate is the same thought as תתלוצצו of Is. 28, 22. It is the mocking derision of and the picking of flaws in the phrases of the prophet that is here referred to.

106. Giesebricht, Jeremias Hand K zum A. T. in loco.

107. The Hebrew text would be היכל יהוה היכל יהוה היכל יהוה שקר המה

108. LXX Ed. Swete. B.

109. Midrash Shir hashirim 1, 1.

110. See Die Salomo Sage in der Semitischen Literatur, Georg Salzberger Berlin—Nikolassee, 1907. Koran, Suras 21, 27, 34, 38. See also Literature in Jewish Encyclopedia, Vol 11 page 444, 446.

111. The numbers as given in the text are vague. The LXX (Swete) has five thousand instead of the three thousand. The counting would presume a copy of some book whose proverbs could be counted, but the whole form of the passage is against this. The numbers are therefore used to indicate indefinite rather than definite number. See Kittel, Die Bücher der Könige, Handkommentar zum A. T. Göttingen 1900. Benzinger, Kurzer hand kommentar zum A. T.

112. See Yalkuṭ Shimoni, in loco.

113. Schechter, Jewish Quarterly Review, Vol 3 pages 682 ff.

Neubauer and Cowley, Original Hebrew of Ecclesiasticus, Introduction; Reifman, Haasif, Vol III.

114. The Greek text of Ben Sira 51, 6 reads as follows: *βασιλει διαβολη γλωσσης αδικον.* The Greek 6a is the Hebrew 5c. Greek has 5a, b. 6a, b, c. The Hebrew has 5abc, 6ab. For the Greek, as above given, the Hebrew has וחצי לשון מרמה for which see Strack who prefers to Jeremiah 9, 7. But the better reference is Ps 120, where the other parallels are found שפתי שקר and לשון מרמה.

115. מאור עינים ומשמיעת אזנים וריח אפים וממשש ידים לטיעת החך והולך רגלים כלם לבעל חיים מצויים יתרון על אלה דבור שפתים לא נמצא לבד באנוש.

The author is here concerned with the praise of חכמה. That, he says, is the distinctive property of man. The function of the five senses (the author adds a sixth—motion) are shared by all creatures, but speech, the means by which חכמה is transmitted is given to man alone. On this see further on page 7 line 2 כי חמשה שערים נמצאים בבעלי חיים ובכולם לא נמצא דרך חכמה

For לטיעת Schechter proposes to read לעיטת. See Genesis 29, 30.

116. See Zunz Gottesdienstliche Vortraege page 320. See also note by D. Kaufman in the Revue des Etudes Juives Vol 4 page 161 and Perles, Revue des Etudes Juives Vol 3, pages 116-118 and Joel, Blicke in die Religionsgeschichte zum Anfang de Zweiten Christlichen Jahrhunderts Breslau and Leipzig 1880. page 74.

The Jerushalmi passge (Talmud Jerushalmi Sanhedrin 28a) reads as follows concerning the ספרים חיצונים,

רבי עקיבא אומר אף הקורא בספרים החיצונים כגון ספרי בן סירא וספרי בן לענה: אבל ספרי המירם וכל ספרים שנכתבו מכאן והילך הקורא בהן כקורא באיגרת :

In the discussion on the same topic in the Babli (Sanhedrin 100b) and touching upon the same Mishnah, it is to be noticed that Ben Sira is mentioned and Ben Laanah is not. The omission is to be accounted for by the possibility that between the time of the two Talmuds Ben Laanah had lost vogue and was no more a vital subject of discussion or illustration. At any rate it would go to show that Ben Laanah whether that be the name of a book or of an author was an early writer or book.

The passage in which Ben Tagla is mentioned is in Koheleth Rabba to 12, 12 and reads as follows:

"ויותר מהמה בני הזהר" מהומה שכל המכניס בתוך ביתו יותר מכ"ד ספרים מהומה הוא מכניס בביתו כגון ספר בן סירא וספר בן תגלא :

Joel above cited thinks that Ben Tagla was an apocalyptic book גלה and assumes that Ben Laanah was of the same nature but the fact that wherever the books are mentioned it is in connection with Ben Sira, whose character is too well defined as a proverbial book, militates against any apocalyptic theory. Fürst (See Jewish Encyclopedia article, Ben Tagla, Ginzberg,) says that Laanah is Apollonius of Thyane and that Tagla is Empedocles. This attempted identification however is too remote. Equally remote and improbable is the identification suggested by Linderman (See Kaufman, above quoted) with Eusebius and Jerome. Perles regards בן תגלא as a mistake for בן תעלא and would see in it the "fox parables."

In the בן לענה he sees the ספרי בלענה the washers books ($\beta\alpha\lambda\alpha\nu\epsilon\acute{o}s$). He reads the text therefore משלי. בן סירא ממשלות בלנאים ממשלות שועלים. But unless we have in the last two real actually current books alluded to, instead of a class of books, as Perles interpretation would make both, the examples (and both are quoted as examples) would not be parallels with Ben Sira. And if ממשלות שועלים refer to a class, there could not be any real valid objection to them. See above on the משלות שועלים of Rabbi Meir and of Jochanan Ben Zaccai.

See also note by D. Kaufman in Revue des Etudes Juives 4, 161 containing a quotation cited by Steinschneider (Hebr. Bibli. VIII, 65.) as being from the עין הקורא of Messer Leon, commenting on the passage in Sanhedrin and Ben Laana as follows:

כגון ספרי יענה ואני ראיתי אותם הספרים שהם חדות והבלים וכמש' הרב בפי המשנה שהם ספרים מלאים תעתועים :

In the absence of more extended mention of either Ben Tagla or Ben Laanah in the sources, and in the further absence of any quotation from either, all that can be warrantably inferred is that from the fashion in which they are mentioned and from the context they must refer to actual books and cannot be merely terms for a class of writings; furthermore they must have been early proverbial collections, hence their appearance with Ben Sira, that they were at one time on the brink of being admitted into the canon, but failing in this they were lost so that the Talmud Babli does not even mention them.

117. See (a) Proverbs 12, 4; 18, 22; 19, 14; 30, 20ff; 5, 15-20; 11, 16; 31, 10-31;

(b) Proverbs 2, 16-19; 5, 2-14; 5, 20ff; 6, 24; 7, 5ff; 11, 22; 19, 13; 21, 9; 25, 24; 22, 14; 23, 7;

Ben Sira 9, 1-9; 12, 14; 19, 2; 25, 8; 25, 13, 17-24; 26, 1-2; 7,23.

118. Strack text of Ben Sira 38, 15. אשר חוטא לפני עושהו יתגבר לפני רופא:

See Smend Die Weisheit des Jesus ben Sirach, Berlin, 1906, p. 342.

Cf. Soferim 15 Halachah 10. טוב שברופאים לגיהנום

119. Strack text 38, 1. רעי רופא לפני צרכו גם אתו חלק אל מאת אל יחכם רופא ומאת מלך ישא משאות דעת רופא תרים ראשו ולפני נדיבים יתיצב :

120. שבעה אין להם חלק לעולם הבא ואלו הן לבלר וסופר וטוב שברופאים ודיין לעירו וקוסם חזן וטבח :

See also the following note in Pesiḳta Rabbati, Ed. Friedmann page 42b אמר ר׳ לוי הפתח שאינו פתוח למצוה פתוח לרופא

The note reads as follows: אמר ר׳ לוי מתלא אמר תרעא דלא פתיח למצוותה יהא פתות לאסייא

See also Ḳiddushin 82a רבי יהודה אומר משמו החמרין רובן רשעים והגמלים רובן כשרין הספנין רובן חסידים, טוב שברופאים לגיהנום והכשר שבטבחים שותפו של עמלק

The phrase concerning the physician is not of the language and style of the rest of the passage and is evidently a quotation—most likely a popular saying.

121. Hebrew Text: וקרוב לשמוע מתת הכסילים זבח but see Kittel, Biblia Hebraica, Leipzig, 1906 and the note that the Syriac had זבח הכסילים.

LXX (Swete B) reads *καὶ ἐγγὺς του ἀκούειν ὑπὲρ δόμα τῶν ἀφρονων θυσία σου* it therefore points to a text which had the same consonants but it read different vowels and had מתת. The Massoretic reading however is better. Barton, Ecclesiastes, International Ciritcal Com. New York 1908. has "and to draw near to obey is better than that fools should give sacrifice." This construction of קרוב used as an infinitive subject is maintained by Nowack, Hand Kommentar in loco. Wildeboer, Kurzer Hand Kommentar, in loco, has the imperative continued through to קרוב "aber man übersetzt besser mit De Jong unter anderung in וקרוב 'Hüte deinen Fuss, so wirst du dem gehorsamsein naher kommen als wenn die Thoren Schlachtopfer bringen." Graetz, Koheleth, Leipzig 1871, in loco takes קרוב as an adjective. Volck, Kurzgefaster Kommentar zum A. T. Nordlingen 1889 in loco, takes it as an infinitive absolute and subject of the clause as does also Hitzig Der Prediger Salomo's Leipzig 1847. The rendering of קרוב as an infinitive has against it that a טוב must be inserted. The second rendering cannot be maintained seeing that וקרוב לשמוע מתת הכסילים זבח is most probably an old selection quoted by the author. We take קרוב therefore as an adjective in the sense of טוב or "near" "pleasing" i. e. to God. Who are the כסילים? Jastrow suggests they are the priests. But that is a modern application and is too harsh a description of the priestly class even for the sceptical writer of Koheleth. The sacrifice is of course a literal sacrifice; the כסילים are those, then, who imagine that through sacrifices alone can they be accounted righteous.

122. Note a similar tradition concerning Hillel in Treatise Soferim 16, 9. as follows:

אמרו עליו על חלל שלא עזב דברי חכמים שלא למד אפילו כל הלשונות אפילו שיחת הרים וגבעות ובקעות שיחת עצים ועשבים שיחת חיות ובהמות שיחת שדים ומשלות :

Index of Passages in the Bible and Apocrypha Quoted or Discussed

II Kings Page

Isaiah

Jeremiah Page

Ezekiel

Hosea

www.ingramcontent.com/pod-product-compliance
Lightning Source LLC
LaVergne TN
LVHW020646100826
845148LV00012B/2351

* 9 7 8 1 5 5 6 3 5 6 4 8 3 *